The Cambridge Introduction to
Shakespeare's Tragedies

Macbeth clutches an imaginary dagger; Hamlet holds up Yorick's skull; Lear enters with Cordelia in his arms. Do these memorable and iconic moments have anything to tell us about the definition of Shakespearean tragedy? Is it in fact helpful to talk about 'Shakespearean tragedy' as a concept, or are there only Shakespearean tragedies? What kind of figure is the tragic hero? Is there always such a figure? What makes some plays more tragic than others? Beginning with a discussion of tragedy before Shakespeare and considering Shakespeare's tragedies chronologically one by one, this book seeks to investigate such questions in a way that highlights both the distinctiveness and the shared concerns of each play within the broad trajectory of Shakespeare's developing exploration of tragic form.

Janette Dillon is Professor of Drama at the School of English, University of Nottingham.

Cambridge Introductions to Literature

This series is designed to introduce students to key topics and authors. Accessible and lively, these introductions will also appeal to readers who want to broaden their understanding of the books and authors they enjoy.

- Ideal for students, teachers, and lecturers
- Concise, yet packed with essential information
- Key suggestions for further reading

Titles in this series:

The Cambridge Introduction to
Shakespeare's Tragedies

JANETTE DILLON

CAMBRIDGE
UNIVERSITY PRESS

CAMBRIDGE UNIVERSITY PRESS
Cambridge, New York, Melbourne, Madrid, Cape Town, Singapore, São Paulo

Cambridge University Press
The Edinburgh Building, Cambridge CB2 8RU, UK

Published in the United States of America by Cambridge University Press, New York

www.cambridge.org
Information on this title: www.cambridge.org/9780521674928

First published 2007

Printed in the United Kingdom at the University Press, Cambridge

A catalogue record for this publication is available from the British Library

Library of Congress cataloguing in publication data
Dillon, Janette, 1953–
The Cambridge introduction to Shakespeare's tragedies / by Janette Dillon.
p. cm. – (Cambridge introductions to literature)
Includes bibliographical references and index.
ISBN 978-0-521-85817-5
ISBN 978-0-521-67492-8 (pbk)
1. Shakespeare, William, 1564–1616 – Tragedies.   I. Title.   II. Series.
PR2983.D55 2007 822.3'3 – dc22

ISBN 978-0-521-85817-5 hardback

ISBN 978-0-521-67492-8 paperback

Contents

Acknowledgements

Quotations from Shakespeare's tragedies, except where otherwise indicated, are from the Arden third series where available, and the Arden second series otherwise. Quotations from Shakespeare's other plays are from *The Riverside Shakespeare*, gen. ed. G. Blakemore Evans, 2nd edn (Boston: Houghton Mifflin, 1997). Since Shakespeare is almost always quoted in modern spelling, I have modernised the spelling of all contemporary quotations for consistency with this practice. The drawing attributed to Henry Peacham, possibly of Shakespeare's *Titus Andronicus*, page 27, is reproduced by permission of the Marquess of Bath.

I am indebted to Brean Hammond for reading the whole typescript in draft, and to the usual suspects for sharing conversations on Shakespearean tragedy. They know who they are. I am grateful too for the support of Sarah Stanton at Cambridge University Press.

Introduction

Imagine that, as in the current vogue of Saturday night British television, you are watching the Top 100 Shakespearean Tragic Moments. What will reach the top five? Macbeth clutching at an imaginary dagger? Lear with Cordelia in his arms? Cleopatra holding the asp to her breast? Juliet falling on Romeo's body? Number one would surely have to be one of two iconic moments from *Hamlet*: 'Alas, poor Yorick' or 'To be or not to be'. Do these moments have anything in common that helps us towards a definition of Shakespearean tragedy? The only more or less common factor is perhaps a relentless focus on the solitary individual; but this may be less an effect of Shakespearean tragedy itself than of a post-Romantic way of reading Shakespearean tragedy almost solely through the lens of the tragic hero. Of course Shakespearean tragedies do have heroes, some more heroic than others, and one or two very hard indeed either to admire or to sympathise with (Coriolanus or Timon, for example). These moments, however, are less individually focused than they may appear to be at first glance. Lear and Juliet are both embracing a lost loved one and Lear is surrounded by other people in that moment; Cleopatra has to struggle to get rid of the clown before she can put the asp to her breast, and Charmian remains at her side for the moment itself; Hamlet is with Horatio and has been exchanging jokes with the gravedigger when the gravedigger throws up Yorick's skull; Hamlet is observed by Claudius, Polonius and Ophelia when he ponders whether to live or die. Only Macbeth is alone when he reaches for the dagger.

Neither Shakespearean tragedy nor earlier Elizabethan tragedy would usually emphasise the individual to the exclusion of the state. Indeed a feature shared by all Shakespeare's tragedies, as well as by most of the tragedies written by Shakespeare's contemporaries, is that their closure depends on a restoration of political order following the central death or deaths of individuals. If we were to focus on the closing scenes of Shakespeare's tragedies rather than those moments that have permeated the collective memory, we would find that the stage is usually full and the focus is on two things: how the tragic hero will be remembered and how the rest will carry on. And if, alternatively, we pick out moments that appear insignificant and are often cut in performance, we will go further towards understanding not only what is distinctive about Shakespearean tragedy but what is distinctive about each tragedy. In chapters that follow, therefore, one approach to be pursued is the close analysis of particular moments, some apparently peripheral, in order to examine how they speak of the play's particular concerns. Characters who appear in one scene only, like Lady Macduff in *Macbeth* or Cornwall's servant in *Lear*, may be as important to the shaping of tragedy as the designated tragic hero.

It is probably neither possible nor desirable to find a one-size-fits-all definition of tragedy, though the attempt is often made.

> Tragedy, then, is an imitation of an action that is serious, complete, and of a certain magnitude; in language embellished with each kind of artistic ornament, the several kinds being found in separate parts of the play; in the form of action, not of narrative; through pity and fear effecting the proper purgation of these emotions.
>
>   . . .
>
>   The Plot, then, is the first principle, and, as it were, the soul of a tragedy: Character holds the second place.
>   Aristotle, *Poetics*, ch. vi

> A tragedy is a story of exceptional calamity leading to the death of a man in high estate.
>   A. C. Bradley, *Shakespearean Tragedy* (1904)

> In aesthetics, tragedy is the quality of experience whereby, in and through some serious collision followed by fatal catastrophe or inner ruin, something valuable in personality becomes manifest, either as sublime or admirable in the hero, or as the triumph of an idea. The situation itself or its portrayal is termed tragedy. The characteristic subjective effect is that of a complex of strongly painful and pleasurable elements existing simultaneously, both of which may be regarded as arising from sympathy.
>   The Internet Encyclopaedia of Philosophy, http://www.iep.utm.edu/t/
>   tragedy.htm

Aristotle heads this selection of definitions because he has been the single most influential thinker on Western tragedy. Yet there are two important caveats in relation to assessing his relevance to Shakespearean tragedy. The first is that Shakespeare, along with most of his contemporaries, almost certainly never read his major work on tragedy, the *Poetics*; and the second is that Aristotle, when he wrote, was describing the Greek tragedy of the fifth century BCE, not prescribing what tragedy should be.

Raymond Williams' view of tragedy is helpful here. He argues that tragedy is specific to particular times and places, always arising out of the precise 'structure of feeling' determining what can be thought and created in that particular time and place.[1] Thus Greek tragedy differs from English medieval tragedy, which in turn differs from Elizabethan tragedy, because historically and culturally specific conditions of being created different possibilities for thinking and writing.

> Our thinking about tragedy is important because it is a point of intersection between tradition and experience, and it would certainly be surprising if the intersection turned out to be a coincidence. Tragedy comes to us, as a word, from the long tradition of European civilization, and it is easy to see this tradition as a continuity in one important way: that so many of the later writers and thinkers have been conscious of the earlier, and have seen themselves as contributing to a common idea or form. Yet 'tradition' and 'continuity', as words, can lead us into a wholly wrong emphasis. When we come to study the tradition, we are immediately aware of change. All we can take quite for granted is the continuity of 'tragedy' as a word. It may well be that there are more important continuities, but we can certainly not begin by assuming them.
>
> Raymond Williams, *Modern Tragedy* (1966)

It makes more sense, then, to ask questions about the particular forms of tragedy we are dealing with than to focus on the broad and reductive question that flattens out difference. In any case, our views of tragedy are now so thoroughly shaped by Shakespeare, that it is almost impossible to explore what we think it is or should be without reference to his plays; thus, arguments about the definition of tragedy *per se* in a post-Shakespearean era often tend towards circularity.

Even the most seemingly simple and uncontentious definitions can be found wanting. When Bradley writes that 'a tragedy is a story of exceptional calamity leading to the death of a man in high estate', he ignores the fact that not all tragedies end in death, though all of Shakespeare's do. Attempts to reduce even Shakespearean tragedy, far less all tragedy, to formulaic definitions are doomed to failure partly by virtue of the fact that they are so reductive.

> All of Shakespeare's tragic heroes have a flawed nature or blind spot that leads to their downfall:
> > for Hamlet it is procrastination
> > for Macbeth it is ambition
> > for Coriolanus and Othello it is pride
>
> RSC website on *King Lear*, 2004–5, http://www.rsc.org.uk/lear/tragedy/tragedies.html

Such formulations distort more than they reveal; and, as Jonathan Bate remarks, talk of a tragic flaw (derived from Aristotle's concept of *hamartia*) is very misleading, since *hamartia*, by Aristotle's account, is 'not a psychological predisposition but an event – not a character trait but a fatal action'.[2]

Though Williams' argument for thinking about tragedy primarily within its historical moment is a very powerful one, some studies have nevertheless usefully made comparisons across huge gaps in historical time. Emily Wilson for example, in a recent study comparing classical and Shakespearean tragedy (without making any argument for continuity or direct influence) shows that the idea of 'overliving', living beyond the point when life has any value, is shared by a select number of classical and Shakespearean tragedies and that this is one reason why death itself is not necessarily the end of every tragedy.

> Tragic overliving often blurs the distinction between life and death. Excessive life is presented as a kind of living death.
>   Emily Wilson, *Mocked With Death* (2004)

Both *King Lear* and *Macbeth*, as Wilson points out, 'use parodic and perverted versions of the Resurrection to suggest the horrors of an unending life in the body', and Macbeth, as he comes to see his own life an endless sequence of repetitions, associates that sense of having lived too long with theatre itself, where the same plays are performed again and again.[3]

For Stephen Booth, the uniting factor of tragedy across time (though his book focuses only on Shakespearean tragedy) is indefinition.

> Tragedy is the word by which the mind designates (and thus in part denies) its helplessness before a concrete, particular, and thus undeniable demonstration of the limits of human understanding . . . the traditional expense of time and effort on defining dramatic tragedy is explicable as an extension of the emergency measure that the word tragedy is itself; the whole subject exists to cope with human nervousness at the fact of indefinition. One can see, too, why some people have wanted to devote themselves to checking particular plays against particulars of Aristotle's formulas. As long as they attempt mastery only of the obviously limited problem they present themselves, they can avoid facing the intellectual limitation of which tragedy is the terrible advertisement. Along with the clown in Othello, they can say, 'To do this is within the compass of man's wit, and therefore I'll attempt the doing of it.'
>   Stephen Booth, *King Lear, Macbeth, Indefinition, and Tragedy* (1983)

It may be possible in this way to reconcile the historical and the transhistorical approaches. If tragedy is a response to indefinition, it is only to be expected that different eras and even different individual writers will respond to that indefinition in distinct and distinctive ways.

Shakespeare's way, this book will argue, was experimental. In each play he set himself new challenges, playing with the idea of tragic form to produce very different effects, though some of the same concerns recur. The aim of the individual chapters that follow will be to explore the range of this experimentation within those changing contexts, giving full weight to the distinctiveness of each play within a developing sense of what the continuities are in Shakespearean tragedy. The plays covered are those that comprise the group named as 'Tragedies' in the First Folio, with the exception of *Cymbeline*, which is tragicomic rather than tragic.[4] Quite how *Cymbeline* found its way into the tragic grouping is unclear. As the last play in the volume, it may simply have been added in at the last minute; or it may be that its focus on a British king gave it a superficial resemblance to *King Lear* and the history plays, several of which have a tragic shape. Indeed, those plays classified as 'Histories' in the Folio are grouped together only because their subject is relatively recent English history and their focus is on English kings. It is notable that Shakespeare's dialogue with history and historical sources in the wider sense is ongoing in a majority of the tragedies. Not only do *King Lear* and *Macbeth* centre respectively on ancient British and Scottish history, but three more tragedies, *Julius Caesar*, *Antony and Cleopatra* and *Coriolanus*, deal with Roman history as mediated through Plutarch; another, *Timon of Athens*, takes a Greek historical subject from Plutarch; and one further one, *Titus Andronicus*, while not following a known historical source, locates its tragedy in ancient Rome.

Troilus and Cressida, printed as *The Tragedy of Troilus and Cressida* in the Folio, between the histories and the tragedies, but not listed in its contents at all, and also dealing with Roman history, is more problematic. Its most prominent vein is satire, a vein that is also visible but nowhere else so dominant, in Shakespeare's other tragedies, and its structure is certainly unlike that of any of his other plays. We might fairly say that it defies generic categorisation. Discussion of *Troilus and Cressida* and some of the history plays would have usefully widened the consideration of what Shakespearean tragedy is, but it would also have cut the available space for discussing each play considered; and this pragmatic reason, more strongly than any reason of principle, has dictated their exclusion.

To attempt to cover even ten plays in a book of this size, in a field where so much has been written, is a daunting task, and readers are bound to feel cheated of all the subjects that are not discussed. Writing about a single Shakespearean tragedy within the context of a book on Shakespeare's tragedies, however, offers a unique opportunity to examine that play both individually and as part of the broad sweep of Shakespeare's development of tragic form, and I have approached the writing with that perspective very much in mind. To speak of Shakespeare's development, moreover, is to include his collaborative development where that is relevant; and at least three of the tragedies, *Titus Andronicus*, *Timon of Athens* and *Macbeth*, have possible links with other dramatists. *Timon of Athens* is now widely agreed to represent a collaboration between Shakespeare and Middleton; evidence for Peele's co-authorship of *Titus Andronicus* is quite strong; and Middleton's hand, perhaps as reviser, is again evident in *Macbeth*.[5] There is no space in a book of this kind to discuss these matters in any detail, but it is important to emphasise that discussing them as 'Shakespearean' should not be taken to imply sole authorship of all the plays. Collaboration was the norm in the theatre of his time, and Shakespeare was relatively unusual in being sole author of so many of his plays.

I explore these plays as part of an ongoing testing of tragic form by a dramatist who was nothing if not innovative, borrowing material from a wide and disparate range of sources, sometimes lifting passages wholesale as they stood, yet always making a new and highly theatrical whole out of the elements he brought together. My aim is above all to open up rather than close down the plays for readers; that is to say, I discuss ways of seeing and reading them, rather than offer closed interpretations. I do not seek to reduce each play to a single, unified meaning, but to suggest to the reader some of the multiple ways in which meanings are produced. I have also aimed throughout to maintain the reader's awareness of the plays as material events in material theatres as well as printed texts in a written tradition. To begin that exploration, then, we must start by looking historically at both the written and performance traditions of tragic theatre before Shakespeare.

Chapter 1

Tragedy before Shakespeare

The First Folio collected edition of Shakespeare's *Works*, published in 1623, seven years after his death, grouped his plays under three headings: comedies, histories and tragedies. To spectators and readers of Shakespeare now, those three terms are so familiar as to be almost impossible to imagine doing without; but this was not the case in 1623, when 'comedy' and 'tragedy' had been terms denoting types of plays for only a century or so in England, and 'history' in this sense, as a dramatic genre, was very new indeed. Samuel Johnson was of the opinion that neither Shakespeare nor '[t]he players, who in their edition divided our author's works into comedies, histories and tragedies, seem . . . to have distinguished the three kinds by any very exact or definite ideas'; and the evidence of the First Folio itself, with its classification of *Cymbeline* as a tragedy and its heading of *Richard III*, grouped with the histories, as *The Tragedy of Richard the Third*, confirms Johnson's view.[1]

The terms 'comedy' and 'tragedy' in English usage were first applied to narrative poems with happy or unhappy endings respectively. (The words are both of Greek origin, reaching English via Old French from Latin.)[2] The earliest citation for both terms in the *Oxford English Dictionary* is from Chaucer's *Troilus and Criseyde*, written before 1388; and Chaucer also offered a definition of 'tragedy' in the Prologue to *The Monk's Tale*.

> Go, litel bok, go, litel myn tragedye,
> Ther God thi makere yet, er that he dye,
> So sende myght to make in som comedye!
> Geoffrey Chaucer, *Troilus and Criseyde*, Book v, lines 1786–8
>
> Tragedie is to seyn a certeyn storie,
> As olde bookes maken us memorie,
> Of hym that stood in greet prosperitee,
> And is yfallen out of heigh degree
> Into myserie, and endeth wrecchedly.
> Geoffrey Chaucer, Prologue to *The Monk's Tale*

'Tragedies' in this period were primarily stories about the falls of princes (sometimes referred to via the Latin as *de casibus* tragedy). The Latin term *tragedia*, as a term describing a form of drama, was no doubt understood by those educated in Latin from their reading of such works as Horace's *Ars Poetica* and commentaries on Terence, but it is not noted in English until the fifteenth century, at which point it still refers to the classical dramatic form.[3]

It was really from about the 1530s that 'comedy' and 'tragedy' began to be used more widely as terms descriptive of dramatic genre, though 'comedy' could still be used to mean simply 'play' for some time after this. 'History', like 'comedy', had a broad general meaning (of 'story') which continued alongside its more specific meanings, and did not begin to become a generic term for a type of drama until the end of the 1590s. Shakespeare's *Henry IV* was published in quarto as *The History of Henry the Fourth* in 1598, at which point the word is hovering somewhere between its earlier and broader senses and the more specific sense which is about to develop. But by about 1600, Shakespeare himself has Polonius describe the actors who come to Elsinore as '[t]he best actors in the world, either for tragedy, comedy, history, pastoral, pastoral-comical, historical-pastoral, tragical-historical, tragical-comical-historical-pastoral, scene individable, or poem unlimited; Seneca cannot be too heavy, nor Plautus too light' (*Hamlet*, 2.2.396–401). The length and overcomplication of the list makes a joke of genre categorisation, but the joke tells us that categorisation according to genre was becoming an increasingly fashionable and complex matter.

Classical influences

Francis Meres, Shakespeare's contemporary, also used Plautus and Seneca as the comparators for Shakespeare's greatness in his own time.

> As Plautus and Seneca are accounted the best for Comedy and Tragedy among the Latins, so Shakespeare among the English is the most excellent in both kinds for the stage.
>   Francis Meres, *Palladis Tamia* (1598)

Shakespeare's classical models, where he followed them, were late Roman plays, not early Greek theatre or theorists; and two of his earliest plays, one comedy and one tragedy (*The Comedy of Errors* (1594) and *Titus Andronicus* (1592)), show him openly imitating these two great predecessors.

The tragedies of Seneca, the first-century Roman dramatist, were far better known throughout Europe in this period than those of the ancient Greek dramatists (fifth century BCE) and affected the writing of English tragedy more substantially than any body of theoretical writing, including Aristotle's. His plays may not have been written for fully staged performance, but they were performed as well as printed in sixteenth-century Europe and shaped the tastes first of elite, and later of popular audiences. The earliest performances of classical plays in England, in the early sixteenth century, were of comedies, which were produced at the court of Henry VIII from about 1518. The earliest recorded performance of a classical tragedy in England was Alexander Nowell's production of Seneca's *Hippolytus* at Westminster School in the mid-1540s, but very few other productions of classical tragedy are known.[4] Seneca's *Troades* was performed in Latin at Trinity College, Cambridge, in 1551–2; translation of his work into English began towards the end of the 1550s; and Thomas Newton's collection of *Seneca His Ten Tragedies* was published in 1581.

Seneca's plays were especially influential in two ways: on violent and sensational content, especially in revenge tragedy, and on the development of an elevated rhetoric, including especially the pronouncement of *sententiae* (moral and universalising statements).[5] These two areas of influence were singled out by the Elizabethan playwright and prose writer Thomas Nashe, who wrote sneeringly of the way dramatists with no Latin education were now turning to 'the endeavours of art' to produce 'Seneca let blood line by line and page by page' and to steal from English translations of Seneca 'many good sentences [*sententiae*], as Blood is a beggar, and so forth . . . whole Hamlets, I should say handfuls of tragical speeches' (Preface to Robert Greene's *Menaphon*, 1589). A further outcome of the revival of classical tragedy was 'the widespread attempt to Christianize classical tragedy – or, rather, to classicize Christian drama', resulting in drama on biblical subjects with 'Seneca's florid diction, five-act structure, and sententious choruses'.[6]

The work of Sophocles and Euripides was familiar only to a tiny elite, mainly via Latin translation, while Aeschylus' tragedies were barely known at all.[7] English productions of Sophocles and Euripides recorded in the sixteenth century were staged privately at Cambridge colleges and the Inns of Court, and sought to turn the plays into quasi-medieval morality plays. John Pickering's *Orestes*, performed at court about 1567, shows this medievalisation of classical material to an extreme degree. In his hands the story of Orestes is punctuated with allegorical moralising and rustic comedy, and the central comic figure of the Vice takes on the allegorical role of Revenge.

As suggested in the Introduction above, however, the classical name most often associated with the study of Shakespeare nowadays, for no very good reason, is Aristotle. Shakespeare almost certainly never read Aristotle, so that, as Alexander Pope put it in the preface to his edition of Shakespeare (1725), 'to judge . . . of Shakespeare by Aristotle's rules is like trying a man by the laws of one country who acted under those of another'. Aristotle's *Poetics* was printed in Latin translation in 1498, but did not become widely known until after the publication of Francesco Robertello's commentary in 1548, and was not translated into English until the eighteenth century. Sixteenth and early seventeenth-century definitions of tragedy available to Shakespeare were mainly quite simple and formulaic.

> *Tragoedia*, A tragedy, being a lofty kind of poetry, and representing personages of great estate, and matter of much trouble, a great broil or stir.
>> Thomas Thomas, Latin dictionary (1587)
>
> *Tragédia*, a tragedy or mournful play being a lofty kind of poetry, and representing personages of great state and matter of much trouble, a great broil or stir: it beginneth prosperously and endeth unfortunately or sometimes doubtfully, and is contrary to a comedy.
>> John Florio, Italian dictionary (1598)
>
> Tragedy. A play or history ending with great sorrow and bloodshed.
>> John Bullokar, English dictionary of hard words (1616)[8]

Though often based, sometimes unwittingly, on Aristotle, they did not generally derive from a direct reading of his *Poetics* but from commentaries such as Robertello's or late Roman mediations of Aristotle's text, often further mediated through subsequent writers. As Dr Johnson, looking back from the middle of the eighteenth century, rather condescendingly summed up:

> Tragedy was not in those times a poem of more general dignity or elevation than comedy; it required only a calamitous conclusion, with which the common criticism of that age was satisfied, whatever lighter pleasure it afforded in its progress.
>> Samuel Johnson, preface to his edition of Shakespeare (1765)

The view that tragedy requires a certain elevation of both style and content and concerns persons of high estate comes from Aristotle, whom Johnson, writing later than Sidney and Shakespeare, certainly did know; but Renaissance writers owed their awareness of such ideas to later Latin writers such as Horace (first century BCE), whose *Art of Poetry* was widely known, and Donatus, a fourth-century commentator on Terence whose work was part of the standard grammar-school curriculum in England.

Tragedies and comedies, saith Donatus, had their beginning *a rebus divinis*, from divine sacrifices. They differ thus: in comedies *turbulenta prima, tranquilla ultima*; in tragedies, *tranquilla prima, turbulenta ultima*: comedies begin in trouble and end in peace; tragedies begin in calms and end in tempest.

Thomas Heywood, *Apology for Actors* (1612)

Donatus' views derive from Aristotle, who states that 'the sequence of events, according to the law of probability or necessity, will admit of a change from bad fortune to good, or from good fortune to bad' (ch. VII); but it is Donatus to whom Heywood has easy access and whom he cites.[9]

Johnson was more or less right on the broad spectrum of early dramatic practice, but some theorists, especially those influenced by classical practice, had a slightly more nuanced understanding of what constituted tragedy than these remarks would suggest. Even if the 'poem' (under which name Johnson includes poetic drama) was not of itself necessarily elevated in style, the idea that tragedy concerned the fall of someone of elevated social station was fairly widespread, and the view that it should teach or improve its audience even more so. Aristotle does not give much emphasis to moral teaching, though he does say that the fall of a bad man is not tragic. It is again Seneca whose moralising bent most directly determines the characteristic Renaissance form of tragedy (as Sidney's praise of *Gorboduc*, p. 14 below, confirms); and the tendency of Elizabethan translators of Seneca was to extend that moralising bent. Jasper Heywood's translation of Seneca's *Thyestes*, for example, adds a final scene in which Thyestes denounces his own crimes and insists on his punishment; and later Elizabethan writers build up tragedy generally from this same moral perspective.[10]

. . . tragedy, that openeth the greatest wounds, and showeth forth the ulcers that are covered with tissue; that maketh kings fear to be tyrants, and tyrants manifest their tyrannical humours; that, with stirring the affects of admiration and commiseration, teacheth the uncertainty of this world, and upon how weak foundations gilden roofs are builded.

Sir Philip Sidney, *Apology for Poetry* (1595)

If we present a tragedy, we include the fatal and abortive ends of such as commit notorious murders, which is aggravated and acted with all the art that may be, to terrify men from the like abhorred practices.

Thomas Heywood, *Apology for Actors* (1612)

Is thy mind noble, and wouldst thou be further stirred up to magnanimity? Behold upon the stage thou mayest see Hercules, Achilles, Alexander, Cæsar, . . . with infinite others . . . animating thee with courage, deterring thee from cowardice.

Thomas Heywood, *Apology for Actors* (1612)

Thomas Heywood, of course, as a dramatist defending the theatre, had a personal stake in playing up the moral usefulness of drama generally.

It is likely that any knowledge Shakespeare may have had of Aristotle's *Poetics* was, like that of most of his contemporaries, highly mediated, derived partly from his reading of grammar-school texts like Donatus, but also perhaps from a reading of Sir Philip Sidney's *Apology for Poetry*, printed in 1595, but circulating in manuscript before Sidney's death in 1586.[11] Even Sidney, whose work shows a stronger trace of Aristotle than that of most of his contemporaries, may have known the *Poetics* only indirectly, through commentaries like those of Robertello and others, and some of his formulations are based on distortions of Aristotle. When he writes that tragedy stirs 'the affects of admiration and commiseration', he draws on a tradition initiated by Robertello in substituting the element of wonder ('admiration') for that of fear in the original Aristotelian dictum. Sir John Harington, if he too is recalling the Aristotelian formulation, distorts it further when he expresses the view that tragedy moves 'nothing but pity or detestation' (*Apology for Ariosto* (1591)).[12] Both share with their contemporaries an overriding concern with the capacity of tragedy to provide moral teaching.

When scholars and teachers lift single words from Aristotle and seek to apply them to Shakespearean tragedy, they therefore risk a double error; for not only is it highly unlikely that Shakespeare had read Aristotle's original statements on these matters, but the processes of translation and excision from context distort the concepts themselves. Thus when critics look for a 'fatal flaw' (a common, and reductive, translation of *hamartia*) in Shakespearean protagonists, or discuss the effect of Shakespearean tragedy in terms of *catharsis* (the idea that the audience is 'purged' by the experience of the play), any illumination produced is more likely to result from the intention of the reader to find it than from an intention on Shakespeare's part to follow Aristotle's theory. As to the supposed 'unities' of time, place and action, which Shakespeare only occasionally followed (in *The Comedy of Errors* and *The Tempest*), and never in his tragedy, these are falsely attributed to Aristotle, who only ever recommended unity of action.[13]

Now, according to our definition, Tragedy is an imitation of an action that is complete, and whole, and of a certain magnitude; for there may be a whole that is wanting in magnitude. A whole is that which has a beginning, a middle, and an end. A beginning is that which does not itself follow anything by causal necessity, but after which something naturally is or comes to be. An end, on the contrary, is that which itself naturally follows some other thing, either by necessity, or as a rule, but has nothing following it. A middle is that which follows something as some other thing follows it. A well constructed plot, therefore, must neither begin nor end at haphazard, but conform to these principles.

Aristotle, *Poetics*, ch. VII

The earliest English tragedy: the mixed tradition

Tragic writing in English did not begin until well after the term itself came into use as the name of a dramatic genre in the 1530s. The earliest extant English tragedy does not appear until around 1560. *Gorboduc* (1562), by Thomas Sackville and Thomas Norton, is usually cited as the earliest English tragedy, but it could have been preceded by Thomas Preston's *King Cambyses* (*c.* 1558–69). These two very different kinds of play represent two identifiable, though cross-fertilising, strands of English tragedy before Shakespeare, the first openly imitating classical style and the second representing a native tradition of vernacular drama. It is notable too that just prior to 1560, two printing events both conducive to the emergence of English tragedy sprang from these two separate strands of literary tradition, classical and native: the earliest English translation of Seneca (Jasper Heywood's translation of *Troas* (or *Troades*) and *The Mirror for Magistrates* (a collection of *de casibus* verse narratives in the medieval tradition in which different speakers each take their turn in recounting the story of their fall from greatness to wretchedness), both printed in 1559.

Nashe's contempt for imitations of Seneca (p. 9 above), expressed in 1589, suggests that this vein of writing had already come to seem somewhat tired by the end of the 1580s, by which time permanent playhouses had been established in London for over twenty years, and some writers and audiences, especially those with a university education, like Nashe, had become rather sophisticated in their expectations. Senecan tragedies nevertheless continued to please popular audiences for many years to come, as Ben Jonson, making fun of such old-fashioned spectators in 1614, pointed out with reference to two of the most enduringly popular Senecan English plays, Thomas Kyd's *Spanish Tragedy* (1585–9) and Shakespeare's *Titus Andronicus* (1592).

> He that will swear *Jeronimo* [*The Spanish Tragedy*] or *Andronicus* are the best plays yet shall pass unexcepted at here as a man whose judgement shows it is constant and hath stood still these five and twenty or thirty years. Though it be an ignorance, it is a virtuous and staid [unchanging] ignorance; and, next to truth, a confirmed error does well.
>
> Ben Jonson, *Bartholomew Fair* (1614), Induction, lines 93–8

When Sackville and Norton first produced the tragedy of *Gorboduc* in 1562, however, it represented a new direction for English tragedy. First performed at the Inner Temple in London, then at Whitehall before the Queen, it was the first English tragedy modelled on classical form, adopting a five-act structure and a unified approach to plot and character. As in Seneca, violence took place offstage and was reported by a messenger.

Other aspects of its dramaturgy, however, drew on vernacular English tradition. Thomas Sackville himself was a contributor to the second edition of *The Mirror for Magistrates* (1563), first published four years before *Gorboduc*, and *Gorboduc* was pioneering and innovative in non-classical as well as classical ways. Its use of dumb-shows before each act, for example, developed an existing visual and emblematic quality in English drama in a new and influential way, and it was the first English drama to use blank verse, which was to become the norm for almost all verse-drama of the Shakespearean period. Its subject matter too was English, contemporary and political. Though it represented a tale of ancient Britain, its early spectators understood that to be a veil for an otherwise direct intervention in the contemporary and highly controversial subject of who was to succeed the unmarried and childless Queen Elizabeth.

> There was also declared how a strange duke, seeing the realm at division, would have taken upon him the crown, but the people would none of it. And many things were said for the succession to put things in certainty.
>
> Anonymous report of the first performance of *Gorboduc*, at the Inner Temple, January 1562

In this way too, it set an important precedent for later English tragedy, which often differed strikingly from its classical predecessors in having precisely that contemporary and political edge.

Notably, Sidney, who had little but scorn for contemporary English theatre, singled out only this play for praise, while criticising it in the same breath for failing to live up to what he saw as the classically prescribed unities.

> Our tragedies and comedies (not without cause cried out against), observing rules neither of honest civility nor of skilful poetry, excepting *Gorboduc* . . . which notwithstanding, as it is full of stately speeches and well-sounding phrases, climbing to the height of Seneca's style, and as full of notable morality, which it doth most delightfully teach, and so obtain the very end of poesy, yet in truth it is very defective in the circumstances, which grieveth me, because it might not remain as an exact model of all tragedies. For it is faulty both in place and time, the two necessary companions of all corporal actions. For where the stage should always represent but one place, and the uttermost time presupposed in it should be, both by Aristotle's precept and common reason, but one day, there is both many days, and many places, inartificially imagined.
>
> Sir Philip Sidney, *Apology for Poetry* (1595)

In Sidney's praise, however, we see again the very sixteenth-century concern to judge drama by its capacity to provide moral teaching. Even those Elizabethans most influenced by classical drama and dramatic theory, like Sidney, Sackville and Norton, were also shaped by native forms of cultural production, and their very reading of a dramatist like Seneca was inevitably partly determined by that cultural position.

Just as elements of the native medieval tradition shaped Elizabethan English classicism, so too did a degree of classicism often seep into native forms of English drama. Preston's *Cambyses*, for example, probably written for touring, with its instructions to potential actors on how to allocate thirty-eight parts among eight players, gave most of its characters classical names, included Venus and Cupid in its *dramatis personae*, and shared its predominant verse-form, the seven-stress line known as the 'fourteener', with Heywood's translations of Seneca. Though it differed from Seneca in putting spectacular violence directly on stage, as opposed to having it reported by a messenger, it had the interest in sensationalism itself in common with Seneca.

> *Smite him in the neck with a sword to signify his death* (line 460)
>
> *Flay him with a false skin* (line 464)
>
> *A little bladder of vinegar pricked . . .*
> Behold, now his blood springs out on the ground (lines 726, 729)
> > Stage directions and speech from Thomas Preston, *King Cambyses*
> > (c. 1558–69)

The use of the term 'tragedy', however, in the first printed edition of this play (*c.* 1569) is much more problematic than in straightforward translations of Seneca. Described on the title page as 'A Lamentable Tragedy, mixed full of pleasant mirth', the running heads (the title as it appears across the top of the pages inside the book) call it 'A Comedy of King Cambyses'. A comedy could, of course, simply mean a play; but the mixing of mirth and sorrow in the title-page text is more explicit and unmistakable, and is quite characteristic of the way a number of early tragedies seem to hedge their bets. *Apius and Virginia* (*c.* 1567), for example, a play that takes its subject matter from classical history, is described on the title page as 'A new Tragical Comedy of Apius and Virginia', while Richard Edwards, whose *Damon and Pythias* (1564–5) is called 'an excellent comedy' on the title page, tells his readers in the prologue that he has decided to call it a 'tragical comedy' because it contains 'matter mixed with mirth and care'.[14]

What emerges, then, from this attempt to separate the two strands of classical and native tradition is their refusal to be wholly separated. Much more typical of English dramatic practice than the classical characteristics of dramatic unity or purity is the mingling of seemingly contradictory modes of dramaturgy.

This is why a quasi-classical theorist like Sidney is so hostile to what he actually sees on the English stage.

> But besides these gross absurdities, how all their plays be neither right tragedies, nor right comedies, mingling kings and clowns, not because the matter so carrieth it, but thrust in the clown by head and shoulders, to play a part in majestical matters, with neither decency nor discretion, so as neither the admiration and commiseration, nor the right sportfulness, is by their mongrel tragi-comedy obtained.
>
> Sir Philip Sidney, *Apology for Poetry* (1595)

It is also what G. K Hunter in our own time is getting at when he writes that '[t]he practice of Elizabethan drama cannot easily be brought into focus for us by the statements of Renaissance literary criticism'.[15] Contemporary theoretical pronouncements about tragedy are more prescriptive than descriptive, tending to narrow down to what tragedy should be than to deal with the full range of what it is.

Johnson, at a distance in time of nearly two centuries from Sidney, is able to maintain a more detached and neutral tone about the gap between classical theory and earlier dramatic practice.

> Shakespeare engaged in dramatic poetry with the world open before him; the rules of the ancients were yet known to few; the public judgment was unformed; he had no example of such fame as might force him upon imitation, nor critics of such authority as might restrain his extravagance.
>
> Samuel Johnson, preface to his edition of Shakespeare (1765)

Indeed he considers the mixture of tones in Shakespeare as a deliberate choice, one that Shakespeare carries out in a masterly way. Mingled dramaturgy, then, as opposed to classical unity, is here perceived as a positive and utterly distinctive quality of Shakespearean drama (though Johnson is not wholly consistent on this point).[16]

> Through all these denominations of the drama, Shakespeare's mode of composition is the same; an interchange of seriousness and merriment, by which the mind is softened at one time and exhilarated at another. But whatever be his purpose, whether to gladden or depress, or to conduct the story without vehemence or emotion, through tracts of easy and familiar dialogue, he never fails to attain his purpose; as he commands us, we laugh or mourn, or sit silent with quiet expectation, in tranquillity without indifference.
>
> Samuel Johnson, preface to his edition of Shakespeare (1765)

As already suggested above, the mixing of seriousness and merriment is by no means peculiar to Shakespeare alone in his own time; but it may be that Johnson is right in attributing the sureness of touch with which it manipulates the audience as distinctively Shakespearean.

Kyd and Marlowe

This sureness of touch, however, came in part from careful observation of his immediate predecessors and contemporaries, most notably Thomas Kyd (1558–94) and Christopher Marlowe (1564–93). Kyd and Marlowe were probably both writing plays for the public theatres before Shakespeare, and Marlowe was born in the same year as Shakespeare, but both died before Shakespeare's career reached its height. Kyd, like many of his own predecessors, brought classical and native elements together in creating a phenomenon altogether new to the English popular stage: revenge tragedy. The plot structure was in some ways Senecan, with its act divisions and its focus on a final bloody climax, and revenge itself had been the impetus underpinning several of the most famous ancient plays (the *Oresteia* and *Medea*, for example). Kyd's *Spanish Tragedy* openly acknowledges its debt to Seneca, quoting directly from the Latin text of his plays, but at the same time it also brings Christian ethics into open collision with the pagan ethos of revenge. Thus, when Hieronimo, father of a murdered son, enters carrying a book and begins to speak with a quotation from the Vulgate (Latin) Bible ('*Vindicta mihi*', or as Hieronimo goes on to interpret God's words, 'Heaven will be revenged of every ill' (3.13.1–2)), it seems that the book he holds must be the Bible, representing his resistance to the impulse to revenge; but as his speech continues he quotes three times from three different tragedies of Seneca, raising the possibility that his book is in fact a collection of Senecan plays, guiding him instead towards the philosophy that '*Per scelus semper tutum est sceleribus iter:*/ Strike, and strike home, where wrong is offered thee' (3.13.6–7).[17] The hovering between contradictory imperatives was in fact to become characteristic of a number of subsequent Elizabethan revenge tragedies, most notably *Hamlet*.

The framing of the action by a 'chorus' of Revenge and the ghost of Andrea ('Here sit we down to see the mystery, / And serve for Chorus in this tragedy' (1.1.90–1)) transforms a specifically classical aspect of tragedy into a framing device that was also to become characteristic of many an Elizabethan tragedy. The continuation of that framing into the device of the play-within-the-play in the last act was to become an even more familiar feature of English drama, highly influential on Shakespeare's dramatic practice. But Kyd does not merely borrow classical structures and plot-devices, he also develops an English version of Senecan high rhetoric, based on the blank verse line introduced to the stage by *Gorboduc*. Realism has no place in this drama. Hieronimo's lament for the death of his son, one of the most famous and frequently quoted speeches of the later Elizabethan theatre, is a formal shaping of aestheticised emotion, as far from the spontaneous outpouring of grief as such a lament could be:

> O eyes, no eyes, but fountains fraught with tears;
> O life, no life, but lively form of death;
> O world, no world, but mass of public wrongs,
> Confused and filled with murder and misdeeds!
>
> (3.2.1–4ff)

Its rhythms, repetitions and sound-patterns lovingly seek to create an iconic expression of grief rather than to imitate its personal or individual expression. When '*a letter falleth*' some twenty-five lines into this speech, informing Hieronimo who killed his son, an audience is not expected to ask how it falls or to complain that this is not very realistic, but to see the hand of providence intervening in the tracing of Hieronimo's course from grief through recognition to revenge.

The dropping of the letter, however, also signals the degree to which Kyd's reworking of classical style is imbued with the native tradition of emblematic props and pictorial stagecraft. Characters typically carry props or perform actions that speak to the audience of their condition or concerns. When Hieronimo enters '*with a poniard in one hand, and a rope in the other*' (3.12.1), the props of the potential suicide signal his despair; when he '*goeth in at one door and comes out at another*' (3.11.7), the disconnected action signals his madness; when he bites out his tongue (4.5.191), he gives literal enactment to his determination never to answer the questions demanded; and other props, such as the scarf that passes from Belimperia to Andrea, to Horatio, back to Belimperia, back to Horatio and finally to Hieronimo, help the spectators to follow the cumulative meaning of the action in a highly focused way.[18] Yet the handling of props within this tragedy is not always tragic in itself. The empty box that Pedringano thinks contains his pardon accumulates an especially grisly irony that casts a bright and almost mocking light on the more tragic deaths of the play. First, the boy who carries the box looks inside it and, finding it empty, imagines how Pedringano will 'flout the gallows, scorn the audience, and descant on the hangman, . . . presuming on his pardon' (3.5.15–17) and soon after this such a scene of jesting is indeed played out up to the very moment when Pedringano is turned off the gallows (3.7.117). Shakespeare learned a great deal from Kyd about how to highlight tragic effects by juxtaposing them with comedy, as Macbeth's porter or the clown who brings Cleopatra the asp demonstrate. Later chapters of this book will show how deeply ingrained and characteristic the admixture of the comic is in Shakespeare's tragedy.

Space is organised as meaningfully as objects in *The Spanish Tragedy*. Some of these effects are clearly scripted, as when Lorenzo and Horatio, later rivals in love, first appear on either side of their prisoner, Balthazar (1.2.109), or when the declaration of love between Horatio and Belimperia is interrupted by the secret appearance of Lorenzo and Balthazar, guided by Pedringano overlooking them, probably from the gallery above the stage (2.2.6). Elsewhere it is merely suggested, as in the possible location of the gallows for Pedringano and perhaps also the curtained scaffold that supports Horatio's dead body for the final spectacle in the same spot as the arbour where Horatio was killed. Kyd's sense of stagecraft in his use of spatial symmetries and ironies is unerring, and Shakespeare's earliest tragedy, *Titus Andronicus*, shows Kyd's influence most clearly. It is not coincidental that Ben Jonson yoked them together as popular legends in 1614 (p. 13 above).

The popularity of *Titus Andronicus* and *The Spanish Tragedy*, both part of the repertoire of the Rose Theatre in the 1590s and beyond, can be supported by the evidence of Philip Henslowe's Diary.[19] So too can the popularity of Marlowe's plays, also part of the Rose's repertoire. His *The Jew of Malta* (*c.* 1589–90), was played thirty-six times at the Rose between 1592 and 1597, more often than any other play recorded in Henslowe's Diary over the same period, and printed editions of *Dr Faustus* continued to appear down to the closing of the theatres in 1642 and beyond. Marlowe's plays show many of the same qualities as Kyd's: a strong grasp of pictorial stagecraft, the same tendency to mix humorous and serious matter and a similar combination of the classical with the native medieval dramatic inheritance. His *Dido, Queen of Carthage* (1585–6), probably written with Nashe, takes its subject from Virgil's *Aeneid*, but adapts it in various ways for a children's company on the English stage. His two-part *Tamburlaine* (1587–8), the story of a Scythian shepherd's rise to a position of earthly power that makes him see himself as either God's rival or his instrument (the play's repeated description of him as the 'scourge of God' is powerfully ambiguous), is strongly pictorial and emblematic in conception, though the aspirations of its hero are expressed through a rhetoric that goes beyond anything in the earlier English tradition. Yet despite its hubristic hero, its soaring verse and its exotic foreign locations, it ends with a scene strongly reminiscent of the Christian morality play, in which Tamburlaine seeks to, but cannot, evade the figure of Death.[20]

Dr Faustus (1588?) is more Christian in subject-matter, but more classical in structure. Like *The Spanish Tragedy*, it frames the action with a version of the classical chorus, which also draws a parallel between the fall of Faustus and that of the classical figure, Icarus. Yet, despite the play's rebellion against the traditional framework of the morality play, which would normally save rather than damn the hero, the closing words of the chorus bring the play's morality seemingly firmly within the fold of the Christian ethos that Faustus has sought to challenge, encouraging the audience

> Only to wonder at unlawful things,
> Whose deepness doth entice such forward wits
> To practise more than Heavenly power permits.
> (Chorus 5, lines 7–9)

The Jew of Malta, by contrast, maintains a cynical distance from all the religions it puts on display, including Christianity, and challenges the boundary between tragedy and comedy even more radically than Marlowe's other plays by undercutting every potentially tragic action with grotesque and farcical elements. (All the early printed editions of Marlowe's plays except *The Massacre at Paris* (1593) have some suggestion of the word 'tragedy' in their titles, though, taken together, they would offer a very challenging definition of the form, and one quite different from Shakespeare's.)[21] Though Barabas, the Jew, dies at the end of the play, his death is presented as a comic parody of the traditional mystery-play descent into hell by having him fall into a rigged stage cauldron of his own design and construction.

Importantly in terms of his influence on Shakespeare, Marlowe also writes a play in the newly fashionable genre of history, where the overlap with tragedy is clear. His *Edward II* (1591–3) primarily focuses on the tragedy of Edward (though the 1597 title page attaches the word 'tragical' to the fall of Mortimer; see note 21 above), showing his fall from greatness into the most abject humiliation. Especially towards the end of the play, characters self-consciously remind the audience of the play's claim to tragic form. Edward, realising that Lightborn has been sent to kill him, says 'I see my tragedy written in thy brows' (5.5.73); following his death, his queen, Isabella, as she sees her son accede to the throne, warns Mortimer, her lover, that their tragedy begins here (5.6.23); and Mortimer, seeing the inevitable approach of punishment by death, voices a very medieval view of tragedy:

> Base Fortune, now I see that in thy wheel
> There is a point to which, when men aspire,
> They tumble headlong down.   (5.6.58–60)

The emergent form of the history play does not, and does not seek to, exclude tragedy. As we saw above, the seeming fixity of the Shakespeare First Folio's categorisations is undermined not only by comparison with the title pages of quarto texts, but within the Folio printing itself. Johnson is again a voice of sanity on the blurring of the categories of tragedy and history:

> History was a series of actions, with no other than chronological succession, independent on [sic] each other, and without any tendency to introduce or regulate the conclusion. It is not always very nicely [scrupulously] distinguished from tragedy. There is not much nearer approach to unity of action in the tragedy of *Antony and Cleopatra*, than in the history of *Richard the Second*. But a history might be continued through many plays; as it had no plan, it had no limits.
>
> Samuel Johnson, preface to his edition of Shakespeare (1765)

Elizabethan tragic practice and theory

> TRAGEDY
> I must have passions that must move the soul,
> Make the heart heavy, and throb within the bosom,
> Extorting tears out of the strictest eyes,
> To rack a thought and strain it to his form,
> Until I rap the senses from their course,
> This is my office.
>
> COMEDY
> How some damn'd tyrant to obtain a crown
> Stabs, hangs, impoisons, smothers, cutteth throats;
> And then a Chorus, too, comes howling in
> And tells us of the worrying of a cat;
> Then, too, a filthy whining ghost,
> Lapt in some foul sheet, or a leather pilch,
> Comes screaming like a pig half stick'd,
> And cries, *Vindicta*! – Revenge, Revenge!
> With that a little resin flasheth forth,
> Like smoke out of a tobacco pipe, or a boy's squib;
> Then comes in two or three like to drovers,
> With tailors' bodkins, stabbing one another,
> Is not this trim? Is not here goodly things?
>
> Induction to *A Warning for Fair Women* (1596–1600)

Thus Comedy parodies the content and stagecraft of a typical Elizabethan tragedy in an induction that sets Tragedy, with whip and knife in hand, in dialogue with Comedy and History in order to determine what kind of play this one shall be. From this reductive listing of the villainies, murders, choruses, ghosts and special effects of tragedy we can see that at least part of its appeal in the popular theatre was to an appetite for sensationalism. But alongside its popular appeal, more learned theorists were also beginning to take seriously the question of how tragedy could give pleasure. Lodovico Castelvetro, whose Italian commentary on Aristotle (the first such commentary to be written in a vernacular language) was published in 1570, was the first to insist on the central importance of pleasure in poetry generally and tragedy more specifically.

> poetry was invented for the sole purpose of providing pleasure and recreation, by which I mean pleasure and recreation to the souls of the common people and the rude multitude.
> Lodovico Castelvetro, *Poetics of Aristotle Translated into the Vernacular and Explicated* (1570)

To his way of thinking, Aristotle's insistence on tragedy's functional aspect of *catharsis* was self-contradictory.

> For if poetry was invented principally for pleasure and not utility, as [Aristotle] demonstrated in discussing poetry in general, why would he have us go to tragedy, which is a species of poetry, principally for its utility? Why not go to it principally for pleasure and disregard utility?
> Lodovico Castelvetro, *Poetics of Aristotle Translated into the Vernacular and Explicated* (1570)

For Sidney, however, writing a few years later in England, the pleasure of tragedy was self-evidently paradoxical. Its very capacity to move spectators to tears was part of the pleasure it gave.[22]

> But how much it can move, Plutarch yieldeth a notable testimony of the abominable tyrant Alexander Pheraeus, from whose eyes a tragedy, well made and represented, drew abundance of tears, who without all pity had murdered infinite numbers, and some of his own blood; so as he that was not ashamed to make matters for tragedies, yet could not resist the sweet violence of a tragedy.
> Sir Philip Sidney, *Apology for Poetry* (1595)

Discussion above of Kyd and Marlowe reveals some of the conceptions of tragedy evident in Elizabethan England soon after the time Sidney was writing. Kyd, as we have seen, was developing a specific subcategory of tragic form, revenge tragedy; while Marlowe was creating very different structures from play to play which call the possibility of a single definition of tragic form very much into question. As noted above, we can barely question our own ideas of tragic form without bringing preconceptions based on Shakespearean tragedy into play; but perhaps it is nevertheless worth testing some of the most commonly avowed features of tragedy against Elizabethan examples of the form. How, for example, does the medieval notion of a fall from high to low feature in Elizabethan tragedies? What kind of figure is the tragic hero? Is there always such a figure?[23] Is he of always of elevated stature? What is it that makes some plays seem more clearly tragic than others?

It is immediately clear that some of these questions make more sense in relation to one play than another. The notion of a fall from high to low, for example, does not map well on to *The Spanish Tragedy* nor on to revenge tragedy generally, nor does it map on to a tragedy of love, like *Dido, Queen of Carthage*. The construing of a fall in Christian terms, as in *Dr Faustus*, or in grotesque and farcical terms, as when Barabas falls into the cauldron in *The Jew of Malta*, makes these plays seem very different from a play like *Edward II*, where a king is reduced by his enemies to imprisonment in a stinking earthly prison. *Tamburlaine*, complicated by being a two-part play which may not have been initially conceived as ending with the hero's death, in any case calls into question the notion of a tragic hero (as does the title-page of *Edward II* by implication, with its identification of the fall of Mortimer as tragic). That Tamburlaine is the hero in an epic sense is not in doubt; but what makes a hero tragic? Tamburlaine is neither of noble birth, nor of elevated moral stature, though he does achieve earthly power and arguably some kind of nobility based on aspiration and outstanding achievement. But what does this kind of hero have in common with Barabas, an outcast Jew who celebrates his own villainy? If we reject both of them as tragic heroes, and cast both plays outside the notion of tragic form, on what basis are we excluding them? What is it that may make an audience feel that these plays may not be tragedies despite the fact that they end with the death of the central protagonist?

Perhaps it is the question of how death is approached, linked with the absence of a moral problematic. In those plays that modern readers and audiences accept more readily as tragedies there is often a problem at the centre, a collision between what the central protagonist, if there is one, wants, thinks, feels and does, and what the society of which he is part allows or approves. Thus Hieronimo in *The Spanish Tragedy*, for example, finds himself overcome with grief and outrage at the murder of his son, but without a way to resolve his situation within the social context of moral and political laws that forbid revenge. Similarly Faustus, driven by an insatiable aspiration for knowledge of the world, collides with religious tenets that condemn such aspiration as a rebellion against a divinely ordained limitation of humanity. A concern with the spiritual dimension of humanity may in itself represent an aspect of what makes us likely to define a play as tragic, since it lends a certain elevation or nobility to the problematic at the centre of the play. Similar questions of definition dog some of Shakespeare's plays, and arguments about his tragedies not infrequently return to the question of how far they are or are not tragic. It will be the task of the chapters that follow to examine what kinds of plays they are.

Chapter 2

Titus Andronicus

Shakespeare's earliest plays were comedies and histories. *The Taming of the Shrew* (1590–1), *The Two Gentlemen of Verona* (1590–1) and *2* and *3 Henry VI* (1591) were probably all written before his first tragedy, *Titus Andronicus*. The first recorded performance of *Titus Andronicus* was at the Rose in January 1594, but it may have been written as early as 1592. Some have argued that it was co-written with George Peele, who wrote the bloody and spectacular *Battle of Alcazar* (1588–9), while others, including Jonathan Bate, the play's most recent Arden editor, believe that the play is wholly by Shakespeare.[1] I do not propose to discuss the question of authorship here, but readers should be aware that the first scene of the play, which I will use below to discuss aspects of stagecraft and scenic form, is considered by some to be wholly or partly by Peele. Since, in any case, I will argue that its strongly rhythmic and symmetrical stagecraft is heavily influenced by Kyd, purity of authorship is not the primary issue here. My concern is with the way the play as a whole operates, and what kind of impact it seeks to make. Whether Shakespeare or a collaborator wrote any given scene, it may be taken that, if there was collaboration, both authors approved, and possibly improved, each other's work. It should also be noted at the start that the scene is the basic unit of construction underpinning a Shakespearean play. The early quarto texts were printed with scene divisions only; a majority of the Folio printed versions have act divisions, but these are not necessarily Shakespeare's.[2]

Titus Andronicus is both a Roman play and a revenge tragedy, indebted to Seneca in style and content, but not obviously modelled on any known source. Its debt to Kyd's *Spanish Tragedy* is equally evident. Both plays show protagonists driven to revenge by the unavailability of justice through any other means, and driven to madness by the experience of grief. Both show acts of barbaric violence set against an implied norm of civil society. And both carefully ceremonialise the performance of revenge. This ceremonial aspect is of particular interest, partly because ritualised or ceremonial action continues to shape the dramaturgy of Shakespeare's later tragedies, though often ironically or oppositionally, and partly because the emphasis on ceremony in *Titus* emphasises the appropriateness of a formal approach to the play. Since character-study, usually within a realist framework, has been such a dominant approach to Shakespearean tragedy over the last two centuries, it is important to note its limitations in approaching such a consciously patterned play as *Titus*.

Scenic form

> *Flourish. Enter the Tribunes [including Marcus Andronicus] and Senators aloft. And then enter [below] Saturninus and his followers at one door, and Bassianus and his followers at the other, with drums and colours.*

Act 1, scene 1 of *Titus* begins with a fanfare of trumpets and a ceremonial entry with drums and flags from three directions, including the stage gallery and the stage doors either side of the tiring house wall.[3] The stage is filled rhythmically by the paced, sequential entrance of each group, and the speeches that follow continue this formality. The voice of the leader of each group is heard in turn. Rome needs a new emperor; Saturninus and Bassianus want to go to war over their opposing claims to the title, but Marcus Andronicus, who holds the crown aloft and speaks at greatest length, speaks on behalf of his brother Titus, whose return from war is imminently expected, and who has been elected emperor by the people of Rome. Saturninus and Bassianus accept his request to dismiss their followers and plead their causes peaceably, and the two groups of soldiers on the main stage exit as formally as they entered, while Saturninus and Bassianus ascend to the stage gallery to join Marcus in the imagined location of the Senate House.

Immediately the scene shifts into a new mode with another symmetrical and even more formally choreographed entry. Here is the detailed stage direction in full:

> *Sound drums and trumpets, and then enter two of Titus' Sons, and then two men bearing a coffin covered with black, then two other Sons, then Titus Andronicus, and then [, as prisoners,] Tamora, the Queen of the Goths, and her [three] sons, [Alarbus,] Chiron and Demetrius, with Aaron the Moor, and others as many as can be. Then set down the coffin and Titus speaks.* (1.1.72)

It is possible that Titus enters in a triumphal chariot, since later in the scene he offers his sword, chariot and prisoners to Saturninus (250–6).[4] (Deborah Warner's production in 1987 had Titus sitting on a horizontal ladder carried by his sons, with the prisoners' heads sticking through between the rungs.) Here, the formality is not based on the symmetry of the two doors but on the hierarchy of a procession, focused on two groups and one striking

The drawing attributed to Henry Peacham, possibly of Shakespeare's
Titus Andronicus, is reproduced by permission of the Marquess of Bath.

anomaly: the Romans, headed by Titus Andronicus, bearing the coffin of his
son (he has in fact lost more than one son in the conflict, but the single coffin
may be emblematic); the Goths, prisoners to the Romans; and Aaron, marked
out as separate by his colour and race and referred to by these attributes in the
stage direction as 'the Moor'.

Both the symmetry of the play's staging and the separateness of the Moor
are visible in the only surviving contemporary sketch possibly depicting a performance from the theatre of this period. The drawing, attributed to Henry
Peacham, shows a prominent horizontal symmetry, with opposing groups of
characters arranged on either side of the central point of Titus' spear.[5] It also
shows clearly the importance of props, stances and gestures, showing Tamora
and her sons kneeling in supplication, Titus responding with a wide gesture,
as though to indicate the impossibility of acceding to her request, his soldiers standing in precisely parallel stances, with their pikes raised, and Aaron
standing proudly, forward and to one side of the kneeling group, his body
showing clear opposition, his sword raised in one hand, and his other hand
gesturing threateningly towards its point. The single piece of clear evidence
for an eyewitness view of the play also responds to the play primarily as
a piece of visual spectacle. A private performance of *Titus* was given at the
house of Sir John Harington at Burley-on-the-Hill in Rutland in January 1596.
The household French tutor, writing to Anthony Bacon, expressed the view
that '*la monstre* [the spectacle]' had more value than '*le sujet* [the subject
matter]'.[6]

Titus' speech following this entrance is a piece of high rhetoric corresponding to the solemnity of the ritual; indeed formal rhetoric is a regular and

recognisable part of the dramaturgy that establishes the pace and elevation of ceremonial moments. Like Hieronimo's lament for his son (p. 18), loss is here formalised and sculpted into a verbal tribute as detached and shapely as a funerary urn. The speech, however, is public where Hieronimo's was private, and Titus' sons have died defending Rome whereas Hieronimo's son was murdered. There is a sense of both necessity and honour about the slow opening of the tomb that will unite them with their many dead brothers, and Titus' direct address to the tomb continues to hold the moment still as the ceremony pursues its stately course:

> O sacred receptacle of my joys,
> Sweet cell of virtue and nobility,
> How many sons hast thou of mine in store
> That thou wilt never render to me more!
>
> (1.1.95–8)

At this precisely timed, ceremonial moment, however, that stillness is instantly disrupted by one of Titus' surviving sons, Lucius, who calls for the death of the noblest of the Goths in return, constructing it as a reciprocal, sacrificial rite, a necessary duty to the dead. Thus death is coolly demanded and agreed to in a formal exchange of question and answer between Titus and his eldest surviving son:

> LUCIUS
> Give us the proudest prisoner of the Goths,
> That we may hew his limbs and on a pile
> *Ad manes fratrum* sacrifice his flesh
> Before this earthly prison of their bones,
> That so the shadows be not unappeased,
> Nor we disturbed with prodigies on earth.
>
> TITUS
> I give him you, the noblest that survives,
> The eldest son of this distressed queen.
>
> (96–103)

This is the cue for Tamora and her sons to kneel to Titus for the life of Alarbus, but Titus' response again emphasises that for himself and the Romans this is a matter not of personal revenge but of religious sacrifice. Her son, he says, is 'marked', and 'die he must / T'appease their groaning shadows that are gone' (128–9). This is the discourse of ancient tragedy, itself performed as part of a religious ritual in Athens, and mediated to the Elizabethans through Seneca, who lived in a society where tragedy was no longer a religious ceremony in itself but retained its discourse of holiness around the shedding of blood for blood.[7] Thus the Messenger recounting Atreus' murder of his brother's sons in Act 4 of Seneca's *Thyestes*, for example, carefully enumerates Atreus' observation of prescribed ritual (decking the altars, binding the children's hands behind their backs and their heads with purple bands, supplying frankincense and holy wine, singing in prayer as he applies the knife). It is crucial to keep 'in all the order due, lest such a mischief great / Should not be ordered well'.[8]

The responses of the Goths, however, supposed barbarians as against the civilisation of Rome, offer the audience a different perspective. For Tamora, this behaviour is 'cruel, irreligious piety'; her son, Chiron, asks 'Was never Scythia half so barbarous?'; and her other son, Demetrius, condemns it outright with the term Titus refuses, as 'sharp revenge' (133–4, 140). There are certainly elements in this play that might be classed as either sacrifice or revenge: the basic premise of death for death; the 'marking' of the victim by his blood-relationship with another; and the manner of death, via ritual dismemberment. Yet, however this first act of violence may be interpreted, there can be no doubt that the terrible excesses of violence to come in the play follow from this refusal of mercy and are conceived from this point onwards as acts of revenge.[9] Though Aaron's cruelties are gratuitous and unmotivated, those of Tamora and her sons are motivated by Titus' calm and implacable insistence on taking her son's life.

Excess and symmetry

The acts of violence in the play are beyond even Seneca and *The Spanish Tragedy* in number and excess. Where most acts of violence take place offstage in characteristic Senecan tragedy, the only one that does so in *Titus* is the rape of Lavinia, and this is anticipated and recalled in such detail as to become at least as strongly embedded in imagination as the staged acts of violence. Yet this excess of violence operates in tension with a highly patterned formality which scripts the acts of violence as carefully and precisely echoic rather than randomly extreme. As outrage is piled upon outrage, staging and rhetoric both deliberately recall the first act of sacrificial slaughter, often in grotesquely distorted ways.

The situation where Titus, in authority over the Gothic prisoners, orders the death of Alarbus, is reversed later in the same scene when Saturninus, now Emperor, sets the prisoners free (1.1.278) and Titus' sons, Lucius and Mutius, help Bassianus to capture Lavinia. As Titus, loyal to Saturninus, starts to follow them, Mutius bars his way, and Titus spontaneously kills him. Moments later, Saturninus appears aloft with Tamora, her sons and Aaron, announcing that he no longer needs Lavinia now that Tamora is to be his queen. Titus' brother and remaining sons plead for Mutius' burial in the family tomb in a highly patterned sequence of speeches which itself becomes another ceremony

The brother and the sons kneel.

MARCUS
Brother, for in that name doth nature plead –

2SON
Father, and in that name doth nature speak –

TITUS
Speak thou no more, if all the rest will speed.

MARCUS
Renowned Titus, more than half my soul –

LUCIUS
Dear father, soul and substance of us all –

MARCUS
Suffer thy brother Marcus to inter
His noble nephew here in virtue's nest,
That died in honour and Lavinia's cause.

(1.1.375–82)

Titus yields to their pleading as he did not yield to Tamora's, and Mutius is interred in the tomb, the second such ceremony in this single extended scene.

The tomb on the Rose stage may have been a free-standing structure, or the actors may have used the discovery space or the trapdoor to indicate it. If they used the trapdoor, another macabre echo would emerge in the spectacular violence of Act 2, when Tamora's sons, Chiron and Demetrius, kill Bassianus and throw him into a deep pit, where the trapdoor is presumably used. (Even without this visual echo, language parallels the pit and the tomb.) Later in the scene, Martius, one of Titus' three remaining sons, falls into the pit, and the terms of his brother's response not only frame the event within a highly ornamental rhetoric that keeps the audience at a distance from an empathetic engagement with Martius' fall, but elaborate on it in a way that highlights it as a different kind of horror, scripting it as a 'mouth' and a 'swallowing womb', an 'unhallowed and bloodstained hole' (2.2.199, 239, 210). This rhetoric in turn grimly figures the offstage action, the rape of Lavinia. When Lavinia returns to the stage it is with her hands cut off and her tongue cut out so that she literally cannot speak the unspeakable violence. (In Peter Brook's 1955 production for the Royal Shakespeare Company, the staging of that violence was famously stylised, with Vivien Leigh's stumps and severed tongue represented by trailing red and white ribbons. Brook's production set a fashion for stylised productions of the play, but Warner's production returned to a more realistic mode of performance.) Again, the rhetoric with which Marcus responds to the sight of Lavinia is alien to modern ears, and is intent on aestheticising her as an object of pity rather than evoking pity in a more directly feeling and realist way:

> Why dost not speak to me?
> Alas, a crimson river of warm blood,
> Like to a bubbling fountain stirred with wind,
> Doth rise and fall between thy rosed lips,
> Coming and going with thy honey breath.
>
> (2.3.21–5)

The speech is prolonged and, like Hieronimo's lament in *The Spanish Tragedy*, paced to give the audience time to contemplate the image of the ravished Lavinia and to linger on the lyrical moments of the speech itself, thus partly transforming the immediate horror of the spectacle into something more iconic and emblematic.

As the next scene (3.1) opens, Tamora's revenge progresses; the processional entry recalls the entries discussed in Act 1; and Titus visibly occupies the position that Tamora occupied in the opening scene: '*Enter the [Tribunes as] Judges and [the] Senators, with Titus' two sons [Quintus and Martius] bound, passing on the stage to the place of execution, and Titus going before pleading.*' Titus' grief, however, is even more extreme. Where Tamora knelt to him he now prostrates himself weeping before her. The procession expresses its rejection of his plea by silently walking past him and off the stage, while Titus himself, by contrast, maintains the elevated rhetoric that characterises so much of this play:

> O earth, I will befriend thee more with rain
> That shall distil from these two ancient ruins
> Than youthful April shall with all his showers.
> In summer's drought I'll drop upon thee still;
> In winter with warm tears I'll melt the snow
> And keep eternal springtime on thy face,
> So thou refuse to drink my dear sons' blood.
>
> (3.1.16–22)

The scene moves further beyond the limits of that opening scene, with its imagined hewing of Alarbus' limbs (1.1.99–102), by bringing on the visibly hewn Lavinia to Titus' sight. Titus responds with grim wordplay on Lavinia's desecrated body ('what accursed hand / Hath made thee handless in thy father's sight?' 3.1.67–8) and threatens to chop off his own hands in response; and within a few lines of this threat Aaron the Moor has persuaded Titus that cutting off his own hand will save the lives of his sons. This takes place on stage, and the scene is wholly structured around acts of dismemberment performed in response to one another. The mocking climax of the sequence is the messenger's return with Titus' hand and the heads of his two sons, demonstrating the uselessness of Titus' sacrifice. The closure consists in a ritual pledging of revenge orchestrated quite specifically by Titus, who instructs the three remaining members of his family to

> circle me about,
> That I may turn me to each one of you,
> And swear unto my soul to right your wrongs.
>
> (276–8)

As they do this he solemnly distributes the three dismembered bodily parts amongst himself, his brother and his daughter, constructing a ritual exit for them in grotesque parody of the familiar formal entry.

Ritual and symmetry organise the excess to the end, and parody is a recurrent element. In the masque of 5.2, when Tamora and her sons play the parts of Revenge, Rape and Murder offering to avenge Titus' wrongs, Tamora's entry as Revenge, in a real or imagined chariot (5.2.47), recalls Titus' victorious entry in 1.1, as does the organisation of space, with figures distributed between the gallery space and the main stage.[10] It also recalls the personification of Revenge and the final masque of *The Spanish Tragedy*, which are the most prominent elements in the aestheticised structuring of the deaths that the revenge form demands. The Grand Guignol effect of the masque is both echoed and extended in the banquet at 5.3, where Titus feeds Tamora the cooked remains of her own sons, stabbing her at the same moment in which he reveals that she has eaten 'the flesh that she herself has bred' (5.3.61). The swift, choreographed sequence of killings again recalls the masque-murders of *The Spanish Tragedy*.

Notably, too, the parallels raise questions about gender and male dominance. Tamora is first presented in a traditionally female posture of supplication, kneeling for her son's life; but from that point on, she takes on a warlike pitilessness that parallels her with Titus, while Titus himself is reduced to begging on his knees; and her adoption of the posture of Revenge in a triumphal chariot appropriates a classically male role. Lavinia, by contrast, becomes a grotesque emblem of female passivity, the particular victim of the masculine Tamora ('O Tamora, thou bearest a woman's face . . . show a woman's pity' (2.2.136, 147). Having defied her father in order to honour her promise to marry Bassianus, she becomes the object of a rape gloried in by the sons of Tamora, who in turn are urged on to excess of violence by the obscenely distorted mother-figure of

Tamora ('The worse to her, the better loved of me' (2.2.167)). From the point of her re-entry, maimed and abused, Lavinia becomes a figure for helplessness, unable even to speak the wrong done to her. These two figurations of the female, as mother-monster and daughter-victim, emulating masculine agency or trapped in varying degrees of passivity, return in different guises throughout Shakespeare's later tragedies.

Comedy and villainy

It is evident from the discussion so far that *Titus* frequently hovers on the brink of comedy or self-parody, even in its apparently most serious moments. As Johnson noted, sometimes with approval and sometimes with distaste (see chapter 1 above), the inclusion of some element of comedy is a feature of Shakespeare's tragedies, and one he shared with several of his contemporaries. In particular, the development of a villainous outsider whose knowingness allows him to collude and joke with the audience begins for Shakespeare here in *Titus Andronicus* and feeds into the later creation of Edmund and Iago. (Julie Taymor's 1999 film sought to represent Aaron's special relationship with the audience by directing him to hold his gaze towards the camera.) Kyd had already developed the duplicitous Machiavellian villain in the figure of Lodovico, and Peele had included a scheming and barbarous Moor, Muly Mahomet, in *The Battle of Alcazar* (1588–9), but it was Marlowe who particularly enhanced the comic potential of the villain in Barabas, the Jew of Malta, developing the intimate and coercive relationship with the audience that was to reach its apogee in Shakespeare's Iago. Thus Aaron, for example, taking Titus' severed hand with him, ostensibly to save the lives of his sons, knows throughout that he has no intention of saving them, jokes with the audience as he goes out with the hand and revels in the pleasure of his own villainy:

> I go, Andronicus, and for thy hand
> Look by and by to have thy sons with thee.
> [*aside*] Their heads I mean. O, how this villainy
> Doth fat me with the very thoughts of it.
> Let fools do good and fair men call for grace,
> Aaron will have his soul black like his face.
>
> (3.1.201–6)

Thus the audience is tossed between Titus' trust and Aaron's glee and back to Titus' prayer, as he kneels to heaven for an outcome that the audience already knows is determined by Aaron. This is not comic relief (a tired and too-easy concept that fails to grasp the real force of Shakespeare's comic effects by reducing them to a merely facile breathing space), but a grim sharpening of the experience of grief and hope within a framework of bitter knowledge.

The play also, again anticipating some of Shakespeare's later tragedies (*Julius Caesar*, *Hamlet*, *Othello* and *Antony and Cleopatra*, for example) brings a clown on for a single brief appearance. A 'clown' in Elizabethan parlance meant primarily a peasant or countryman, but was widening by this time to denote a figure of comedy in drama, whether by accident or intention (though 'fool' is the preferred term for a figure who knowingly and wittily initiates comedy). The comedy of this appearance links directly to the earlier part of the scene, which has shown Titus, maddened by grief and injustice, gathering his kinsmen together to shoot arrows bearing letters to the gods petitioning them 'To send down Justice for to wreak our wrongs' (4.3.52). When the clown enters, bearing a basket with two pigeons in it, Titus mistakes him for a messenger bearing a reply from Jupiter. The exchange between them is comic in a painful way that points up Titus' delusion and suffering, and that comic agony is further stretched as Titus seizes another seeming opportunity to press his cause by giving the Clown a letter to deliver to the Emperor along with the pigeons, as though they are a gift from Titus. When the Clown obligingly carries out Titus' request, his humane response to Titus' plight is immediately contrasted with the Emperor's inhumane response to the Clown. As in the scene of Pedringano's execution in *The Spanish Tragedy*, comedy and wordplay continue up to the very end, persisting to the point of death:

> CLOWN
> I have brought you a letter and a couple of pigeons here.
> [*Saturninus*] *reads the letter.*
>
> SATURNINUS
> Go, take him away and hang him presently!
>
> CLOWN
> How much money must I have?
>
> TAMORA
> Come, sirrah, you must be hanged.
>
> CLOWN
> Hanged, by'Lady? Then I have brought up a neck to a fair end.
> (4.4.43–8)

The joking serves again to highlight the random destructiveness of those in authority in this disordered state.

Core scene: 3.2

This play fits various definitions of tragedy outlined in chapter 1, and in this it is like the other Shakespearean plays that will be examined here, all of which fit some of the traditional definitions in varying ways. But what, we may ask, is both tragic and distinctive about this or any other play? In order to try to answer this question for each play, every chapter in this book will pause to focus on one scene or extract in some detail, seeking to analyse both the distinctiveness of the play and its continuities with other Shakespearean tragedy through it. Here I focus on the scene in which Marcus kills a fly (3.2), a scene only in the Folio text but all the more interesting to isolate for study for that reason, since it is thus inherently detachable to a degree, and Shakespeare may have inserted it at some point after first composition. The setting is one that was to become familiar in Shakespearean tragedy and perhaps arises out of a familiar dumb-show on the earlier Elizabethan stage: a banquet.[11] It is distinctive of this play first in focusing so strongly on gesture and stage picture. Titus' opening speech laments the fact that he and Lavinia cannot adopt the classic pose of grief (with folded arms) as Marcus does, since they lack hands; but, he insists, he can use his remaining hand to beat down his grief when it threatens to overwhelm him:

> This poor right hand of mine
> Is left to tyrannize upon my breast,
> Who, when my heart, all mad with misery,
> Beats in this hollow prison of my flesh,
> Then thus I thump it down.   (7–11)

He expresses his pity for Lavinia (herself a 'map', or visible epitome, 'of woe' (12)) as the pity of the one-handed man for one who lacks even a single hand to still the beating of her outraged heart. Both the expression of feeling via the body and the verbal insistence on stage picture are characteristic of this play, as we have seen, and Titus speaks at length here of his determination to improve his ability to read the 'alphabet' of Lavinia's signs (44). There is irony here too in the anticipation of the next scene, where Lavinia, via a book and a stick, with which she will write using her mouth and her stumps to guide it, will reveal more fully the nature of the wrong done to her; and the irony is also characteristic of the way effects of horror and pathos are drawn out and dwelt upon in this play.

So too is the extended and elevated speech. Yet sometimes the language, though more extended than modern taste would normally allow, can be quite

simple in its vocabulary, as in Titus' advice to Lavinia on how to deal with her
unruly heart:

> Wound it with sighing, girl, kill it with groans,
> Or get some little knife between thy teeth
> And just against thy heart make thou a hole,
> That all the tears that thy poor eyes let fall
> May run into that sink, and, soaking in,
> Drown the lamenting fool in sea-salt tears.
>
> (15–20)

The address to Lavinia here as 'girl' and 'fool' has a simple intimacy and direct-
ness that are in tension with the sheer length of the speech. Intensifying this
intimacy and its pathos is the presence of Titus' grandson, who weeps 'to see
his grandsire's heaviness' and begs him to leave his 'bitter deep laments' and
'Make my aunt merry with some pleasing tale' (46–9).

It is at this moment, threatening to spill over into pure sentimentality, that
Marcus interrupts the scene with violent action, striking at one of the dishes
with his knife. (In Taymor's film it is the boy, Lucius, who kills the fly, and
the scene turns on that knife-edge from threatened violence to laughter and
familial bonding.) Titus' response is instant and unbalanced, but focuses the
tragedy of the play with both comedy and passion simultaneously:

> TITUS ANDRONICUS
> Out on thee, murderer. Thou kill'st my heart.
> Mine eyes are cloyed with view of tyranny;
> A deed of death done on the innocent
> Becomes not Titus' brother. Get thee gone;
> I see thou art not for my company.
>
> MARCUS ANDRONICUS
> Alas, my lord, I have but killed a fly.
>
> TITUS ANDRONICUS
> 'But'?
> How if that fly had a father and a mother?
> How would he hang his slender gilded wings
> And buzz lamenting doings in the air.
> Poor harmless fly,
> That with his pretty buzzing melody
> Came here to make us merry, and thou hast killed him.
>
> (54–66)[12]

Titus' strength of feeling regarding the death of a fly, his whimsical imagining
of the fly as having parents and good intentions, becomes an emblem of the

cruelty of death and the grief it leaves behind. For Jane Howell, directing the BBC television production of the play in 1985, that plaintive cry represented the play's 'depth of passion and philosophy'.[13]

Marcus' quick-thinking reply:

> Pardon me, sir, it was a black ill-favoured fly,
> Like to the empress' Moor. Therefore I killed him
>
> (67–8)

is exactly the right response to distract Titus, whose childlike change of aspect at this news paves the way for Lear's sudden changes of mood in his madness. Childlike though Titus' sudden turn to violence is, however, it is also reminiscent of his mercilessness towards Tamora, and as such functions to remind the audience that he has himself unleashed some of the violence now desecrating his own family.

The scene closes with a moment that not only anticipates the functional importance of books in the next scene, but marks a characteristically Shakespearean pause for still and engaged contemplation of the meaning of events:

> TITUS
>   Lavinia, go with me;
> I'll to thy closet and go read with thee
> Sad stories chanced in the times of old.
> Come, boy, and go with me; thy sight is young,
> And thou shalt read when mine begin to dazzle.
>
> (82–6)

Shakespeare often directs the audience to think about his plays as part of the long tradition of story-telling at moments that are especially sharply felt. Richard II, pondering his own fall, says, more or less to himself:

> For God's sake let us sit upon the ground
> And tell sad stories of the death of kings;
>
> (*Richard II*, 3.2.155–6)

Hermione, in *The Winter's Tale*, asks her young son Mamillius to tell them a tale, and he tells her: 'A sad tale's best for winter' (2.1.25); Lear, reconciled with Cordelia, imagines a future together in prison, where they will

>   live,
> And pray, and sing, and tell old tales, and laugh
> At gilded butterflies.
>
> (*King Lear*, 5.3.11–13)

With the exception of *Richard II*, these are moments when either joy is threatened by tragedy or tragedy is shot through with joy. A vision of '[t]he web of our life' as 'a mingled yarn' (*All's Well That Ends Well*, 4.3.71) is characteristically Shakespearean, giving a particular edge of both yearning and affirmation to his tragedy.

Restoration of order

Titus Andronicus is not the tragedy of one man or even of one family, but of Rome. Despite the fact that twentieth-century criticism has concentrated so relentlessly on the individual in Shakespeare's tragedies, none of his tragedies is about the tragic hero alone, nor do all of them focus to the same degree upon a single protagonist. All are concerned with the well-being of the state, and the Roman tragedies especially foreground political questions. *Titus* is not usually grouped with the later Roman plays, and indeed differs notably from them, especially in adopting a Senecan model and a revenge structure; but they do share a concern with questions of government and the struggle for power.[14] The question of the succession was a pressing one in England in 1592, where Queen Elizabeth, now almost sixty years of age, had not yet named a successor. (As the discussion of *Gorboduc* in chapter 1 showed, the succession was a matter of discussion and concern almost as soon as Elizabeth came to the throne.) Imperial Rome represented a relatively safe fictional vehicle for dramatising sensitive political issues surrounding the succession to a monarch without an heir, and allowed an audience to think about such issues as primogeniture, election and the abuse of power at a time when the approaching end of Elizabeth's reign loomed large. Rome has lost an emperor at the start of *Titus Andronicus*, when the question of who will succeed him is the question that opens the play, and it again loses an emperor in the rapid sequence of deaths at Titus' last banquet.[15]

But the play continues for 135 lines beyond the multiple deaths of the banquet, since the tragedy, typically for Shakespeare, is not completed by the death of the hero, but must reach a point where order is restored to the wounded state. Again, echo and symmetry obtrude in the organisation of stage space. Just as Marcus entered '*aloft*' with the crown in the play's first scene, to offer a resolution to the rival threats of Saturninus and Bassianus as claimants to the imperial crown, so, immediately following the deaths of Tamora, Titus and Saturninus, Marcus and Lucius ascend into the gallery to address the Romans on

> how to knit again
> This scattered corn into one mutual sheaf,
> These broken limbs again into one body.
> (5.3.69–71)[16]

The working out of resolution beyond the point of the major deaths in the play takes longer than it usually does in Shakespeare's later tragedies, and Lucius is scripted to 'tell the tale' of the terrible events that have taken place to the people at large (5.3.93), though Marcus completes it. These two present themselves as appropriate leaders of the state by offering themselves freely to the Romans to be judged and receiving 'The common voice' in favour of Lucius as emperor (5.3.139). (Shakespeare was to turn much later, in *Coriolanus*, to explore the struggle of a man unwilling to be judged by the people in this way.)

Part of what extends the play so long beyond the point of death is again its tendency towards ritual. Once Lucius is acclaimed as Rome's new emperor, he and Marcus descend from the gallery (probably ceremonially, to a long flourish, as Bate's stage direction suggests), and each in turn honours and kisses Titus' dead body. The moment of pause discussed in the fly scene above is reworked as Lucius turns to his son and reminds him of the times his grandfather danced and held him on his knee, told him stories, and bid him 'bear his pretty tales in mind / And talk of them when he was dead and gone' (5.3.164–5). Unusually, though not uniquely, among Shakespeare's tragedies, the play closes with a focus on wickedness and punishment. Lucius proclaims Aaron's punishment to be buried breast-deep in earth and starved to death; Aaron himself defies all repentance; and Tamora's body is condemned to be thrown forth to beasts and birds of prey. The horror of the absence of funeral rites is emphasised by contrast with their importance in the early scenes.[17] The final rhyming couplet, so often a feature of closure in Shakespeare's plays, intensifies the tension between pity and pitilessness by rhyming on the same word, a poetic device much admired in this period:

> Her life was beastly and devoid of pity,
> And being dead, let birds on her take pity.
>
> (5.3.198–9)

Though pity has been one of the responses required of the spectators at different points throughout the play, it is emphatically banished in these closing moments, where the focus is upon the completion of revenge, no longer seized by the individual but finally ordered by the state.

Chapter 3

Romeo and Juliet

By the time Shakespeare came to write *Romeo and Juliet*, around 1595, he was a sharer with the Lord Chamberlain's Men, established as one of two companies licensed to play in London between 1594 and 1600. He was to write for this company, which became the King's Men when James VI and I came to the English throne in 1603, for the rest of his working life, writing on average two plays a year for them. The Rose, where *Titus Andronicus* was produced, was to become the resident playhouse of the other premier playing company in England, the Admiral's Men, while the Chamberlain's Men, up to 1599, played first at the Theatre (until April 1597) and then at the Curtain, both in Shoreditch. *Romeo and Juliet* could have been produced in one or both of these playhouses.

This tragedy could scarcely be more different from *Titus Andronicus*. It is also very different both from any of Shakespeare's other tragedies and, in its totality, from anything that has gone before it on the English stage, though various influences are visible, including those of Marlowe and Lyly, the most notable writer of plays centring on romantic love before Shakespeare. Lyly, however, was a writer of comedy; and many critics have noted the way *Romeo and Juliet* feels more like a comedy that just misses resolution than a tragedy. In both subject matter and structure it resembles Shakespeare's comedies of the 1590s, like *The Merchant of Venice* (1596–7) and *Much Ado About Nothing* (1598), where tragedy seems close but is averted. Its strongly lyrical mode, however, is reminiscent of the non-dramatic poetry Shakespeare was writing in the earlier 1590s (*Venus and Adonis* (1592–3) and *The Rape of Lucrece* (1593–4)) and also of the tragic history of *Richard II* (1595). Like *Titus*, it is highly formal, but its symmetry is less stage-based and pictorial than that of *Titus*, and more a matter of verbal and thematic patterning, as we shall explore further below.

Chorus

Romeo and Juliet, unlike any other of Shakespeare's tragedies, opens with a chorus. This means that from the start of the play we know the outcome:

Romeo and Juliet are 'star-cross'd lovers'; their love is 'death-mark'd' (Chorus 1.6, 9). As with Marlowe's *Faustus* or Kyd's *Spanish Tragedy* (where Revenge and the ghost of Andrea frame the drama in ways partly similar to a chorus), the chorus makes the audience view every scene from within the awareness that a tragic shape is being worked out. Love leads to death from the start of this play, so that tragic closure is a given. The Chorus itself appears only once again, at the start of Act 2, but choric forms of utterance pervade the play, often voiced by the lovers themselves. Thus, for example, Romeo, faced with Mercutio's murder on the day of his marriage to Juliet, sees the wider significance of his action in the moment before he kills Tybalt:

> This day's black fate on mo days doth depend:
> This but begins the woe others must end.
>
> (3.1.121–2)

and Juliet, seeing Romeo climb down from her chamber window after their single night together, has a sudden vision of how their love will end:

> Methinks I see thee, now thou art so low,
> As one dead in the bottom of a tomb.
>
> (3.5.55–6)

Friar Lawrence is often a choric figure, pronouncing on the danger of this rush of love:

> Wisely and slow; they stumble that run fast.
>
> (2.3.90)

> These violent delights have violent ends
> And in their triumph die, like fire and powder,
> Which as they kiss consume;
>
> (2.6.9–11)

and his perspective highlights the moralising aspect which was noted in chapter 1 as such a widespread feature of Elizabethan tragedy. As Sasha Roberts has shown, Friar Lawrence's words of wisdom represent precisely the kind of *sententiae* that Elizabethan and Jacobean readers liked to extract from the plays they read, and the habits of such readers should alert us to differences between the way we now read Shakespeare's plays and the way his contemporaries read them.[1]

Choric comments in the play, however, are not uniformly moralising. Benvolio's remark at the start of the scene in which Mercutio and Tybalt meet their deaths has a choric aspect which focuses more strongly on inevitability than on good or bad behaviour: 'For now these hot days is the mad blood stirring'

(3.1.4). And throughout the play this emphasis on fatedness is held in tension with an emphasis on unlucky accident. Fortune, whom both the lovers see as framing their love, combines the randomness of chance with the uselessness of struggle.[2]

> ROMEO
> O, I am fortune's fool
>   (3.1.138)

> JULIET
> O Fortune, Fortune! All men call thee fickle;
> If thou art fickle, what dost thou with him
> That is renown'd for faith? Be fickle, Fortune,
> For then I hope thou wilt not keep him long,
> But send him back.   (3.5.60–4)

But the uselessness of struggle leaves the lovers as victims rather than heroes of their tragedy. As they are barely responsible for the events that combine to bring their love to death, so, if they achieve tragic stature, it is as icons of young love brought to a sudden end rather than as suffering or heroic individuals. The tragedy here is death itself, the cutting off of life just as it seems to reach the height of human happiness, not the combination of death with a very particular experience or endurance of life.

One of the effects of the pervasive choric perspective is to wrap up this love story as precisely that: a story. Though we see and are involved in the private and personal interaction between the lovers, we are also regularly encouraged to draw back from empathetic engagement and to see their story as exemplary and instructive. It is with this perspective that the play closes, following the reconciliation of the Montagues and Capulets. The Prince's moralising speech is the theatrical equivalent of the camera shot that widens and pulls away, letting us know that the fictional world is closing:

> A glooming peace this morning with it brings:
> The sun, for sorrow, will not show his head.
> Go hence to have more talk of these sad things.
> Some shall be pardon'd, and some punished,
> For never was a story of more woe
> Than this of Juliet and her Romeo.
>   (5.3.304–9)

It helps us cross the threshold between the play and the here-and-now.

'Two households both alike in dignity'

The first theme of the first chorus is the feud. From the start we are told that it is because the lovers take their life from 'the fatal loins' of 'two foes' that they are 'star-crossed' (Chorus 1.5–6). This is one of the things Baz Luhrmann's film version (1996) conveys so well. Both the glamour and the horror of the feud, its terrible, exciting and all-consuming violence, are presented so forcefully in the opening scene in the petrol station that we understand at once how fully this social situation encases and determines the love that seeks to ignore it. The collision in this play is not just between Montagues and Capulets, two rival families, but between two worlds and two ways of being: the world of the feud in which every encounter is tense, risky, noisy and potentially violent, and the world of love in which we first find Romeo, private, withdrawn, lyrical, sighing, apart, 'With tears augmenting the fresh morning's dew, / Adding to clouds more clouds with his deep sighs' (1.1.130–1). He is quite simply not there during the first furious encounter between Montagues and Capulets; and when he arrives after the rush of violence is over, his first words call attention to how differently time passes in his world: 'Ay me, sad hours seem long' (1.1.159). His continuing mode of speech shows him wrapped in an excess of words, shaped in carefully constructed symmetries and antitheses, which is totally at odds with the excess of violence in the world he now enters:

> Here's much to do with hate, but more with love.
> Why then, O brawling love, O loving hate,
> O anything of nothing first create!
> O heavy lightness, serious vanity,
> Misshapen chaos of well-seeming forms!
> Feather of lead, bright smoke, cold fire, sick health,
> Still-waking sleep, that is not what it is!
> This love feel I that feel no love in this.
>
> (1.1.173–80)

Only his sudden awareness that his friends are laughing at him interrupts this absurd monologue of self-indulgence.

Juliet is also introduced as somewhat at odds with her world, though not in the same way as Romeo. As a young girl she is more sheltered than Romeo, not free to come and go outside the household in the company of friends, but closely kept within the family, always in the company of mother, father or nurse. Like him, nevertheless, she sees the world in a different way from those around her. Where he is mooning after Rosaline while his friends are feuding and fighting, she finds herself suddenly at odds with her family as they take the view that it is time for her to marry. There is thus a symmetry between the lovers from the outset. Both find themselves out of step with the world that surrounds them, and both are looking to withdraw from the noise and pressure of their surroundings. Luhrmann's film gives us this symmetry visually, by showing Romeo and Juliet both literally in a different element from their surroundings. When we first see Romeo he is sitting quietly alone, looking out over water. When we first see Juliet, her head is immersed in water while all around her her mother and nurse move too loud and too fast. From then on, water is their shared element throughout; it is the world of love that they try to occupy as though the louder, more riotous world were not really there. Romeo at the Capulet ball also immerses his face in water; the two first catch sight of each other through the water in a fish-tank; the traditional 'balcony' scene is played in a swimming pool; and when Romeo leaves Juliet for the last time he jumps again into the pool. The water, at first the private world of love, becomes the world of death that love determines.

Both the separateness of and the symmetry between the lovers is fully supported by the evidence of the play. It is germane to the shared sonnet of their first meeting (discussed further below) and becomes even more prominent after the two are married. When Romeo is banished from Verona for killing Tybalt we hear Juliet's obsessive repetition of the word 'banished' in one scene (3.2.112–26) and Romeo's even more extended repetition of it in the next (3.3.12–70); and when Juliet's Nurse comes in to find Romeo lying 'on the ground, with his own tears made drunk', she reports that Juliet too is reduced to prostrate weeping (3.3. 83, 98–101). Awareness of this symmetry underlines two important aspects of the play: first, that it does not centre on a single 'tragic hero'; and second, that there is a balance between male and female which is shared by only one other Shakespearean tragedy, *Antony and Cleopatra*. Indeed the very names of these two tragedies flag up, by comparison with those named for a single protagonist, the spreading of the tragic centre across two protagonists.

Comparison with *Titus Andronicus*, also a play without a strong focus on a single tragic hero, and *Richard II* or *Richard III*, tragic or quasi-tragic histories with a very strong focus on such a single figure, but all very male plays, emphatically situated in male-oriented worlds, highlights the experimental nature of Shakespeare's approach to tragedy. Though parallels do exist between these plays, in particular a strong parallel between the lyricism of *Richard II* and of *Romeo and Juliet*, there is little similarity across their structure or across those areas that might constitute the centre of their claims to be tragic. Where *Richard II* clearly aims to depict Richard himself as partly responsible, by nature of the kind of man and king he is, for his own fall from power, and to direct the audience to experience the tragedy at least partly as Richard's own personal tragedy,

Romeo and Juliet shows the tragic outcome of the play as determined not by any fault of either named protagonist but by necessity. And where *Titus* has its villain, Aaron, while *Richard III* makes the villain and the central protagonist one and the same, the only villain in *Romeo and Juliet* is the feud.

The strength of Juliet's role is one of the features that leads critics to compare it with Shakespeare's comedies, where women are regularly stronger, franker and at least as assertive as, if not more assertive than, their male lovers. Nor is it only Juliet who gives the play a strong female presence. The Nurse has the dominant comic role; Juliet's mother has an important part to play; and between them these three create the sense of a female world in which women find a way of being that is quite separate and different from the way most of the men operate in the play, building up the family as a power-centre, opposing rival power-centres, directing their wives and daughters to fulfil these power-centred objectives. Capulet's violence against Juliet when she opposes his wish to marry her to Paris is excessive:

> An you be mine, I'll give you to my friend;
> And you be not, hang! Beg! Starve! Die in the streets!
> (3.5.191–2)

and intervention by the Nurse and Lady Capulet underline its excessiveness.

Against this, Romeo's softer manner, his unwillingness to be part of the feud even before he falls in love with Juliet, but all the more so after he marries her, is seen, even by Romeo himself, as a loss of masculinity:

> O sweet Juliet,
> Thy beauty hath made me effeminate
> And in my temper soften'd valour's steel.
> (3.1.115–17)

Even the Friar, who also stands apart from violence of the male world of Verona, questions Romeo's manhood:

> Art thou a man? Thy form cries out thou art.
> Thy tears are womanish, thy wild acts denote
> The unreasonable fury of a beast.
> (3.3.108–10)

Juliet, on the other hand, shows extraordinary boldness for a young girl not quite fourteen, first in the immodesty, by standards of the time, of her open confessions of love and desire for Romeo, and later in the courage of her resolution to take the Friar's potion. Her long soliloquy in Act 4, scene 3 before swallowing the draught is designed to make the audience feel her fear and thus recognise her courage in overcoming it.

Comedy

Romeo and Juliet, as noted above, is unlike Shakespeare's other tragedies in opening with a chorus. It is also innovative in opening the first scene of the play proper with clowning. The opening conversation between Sampson and Gregory, like the opening chorus, highlights the major themes of the play, but it does so humorously, as wordplay takes the pair from how to deal with insults and how to establish superiority when confronted with 'a dog of the house of Montague' (1.1.7) to how to take women's maidenheads. Already this opening scene sets out to open up a double perspective on the two most serious matters of the play: the feud and romantic love. Both are made objects of fun at a point where only the fourteen-line chorus (a sonnet) has introduced them seriously.

The sequence of violence in this scene is comical but also instructive. We are first shown Sampson and Gregory puffing up their own forcefulness and masculinity in an imaginary encounter with a Montague; two Montague serving men enter, which allows us to see the comic mix of false bravado and cowardice that actually ensues, with Sampson first trying to push Gregory into starting the quarrel, then biting his own thumb, only to deny that he in fact bites it *at* the Montagues. But the ridiculous and trivial exchange of insults swiftly blows up into real fighting, others are drawn into the brawl and only the appearance of the Prince brings it to a close. We see how quickly complete triviality escalates into serious violence in this environment; and we see too how simultaneously absurd and dangerous it is. The play's oppositions are not just between the two worlds of two households, two genders, and two ways of being (feuding and loving), but between two different ways of seeing the world, one comic and one serious.

Relations between the sexes, by contrast with the feud, are treated with continuous comic distance in this scene. Not until Romeo and Juliet meet is love presented with true, if intermittent, seriousness. The comic distance here in this opening scene varies between the easy obscenities of Gregory and Sampson's bragging talk and the exaggerated posturing of the love-struck Romeo, whose friends cannot help but laugh at him, but it never takes up the thread of terrible seriousness already indicated in the Chorus' talk of 'death-mark'd love'. As with the feud, there are conflicting ways of seeing the world of love, but only the reductive one is evident here. The intercutting of these opposing perspectives, nevertheless, is a hallmark of the play. The cynical, knowing dismissal of love continues to threaten its high seriousness throughout.

This is done in a daring and risky way, so that the intensity of this love is repeatedly punctured by obscenity, cynicism or absurdity. Immediately after Romeo has visited the Friar to ask to be married to Juliet that very day, the scene turns to Mercutio and Benvolio joking about great lovers of the past and hinting at Romeo's sexual exertions with Rosaline; when the Nurse arrives to deliver Juliet's message to Romeo, Mercutio greets her with random sexual innuendo; and when Romeo tries to convey his own seriousness to her, she voices the fear that his intention is to 'deal double' with Juliet rather than to marry her (2.4.166). Even in scenes where the clowns and jokers are absent, comedy is never far away. Romeo's prostration following his sentence of banishment, for example, verges on the comic, and the self-consciousness of his pose in speaking to the Friar from this position takes it right to the edge:

> Wert thou as young as I, Juliet thy love,
> An hour but married, Tybalt murdered,
> Doting like me, and like me banished,
> Then mightst thou speak, then mightst thou tear thy hair
> And fall upon the ground as I do now,
> Taking the measure of an unmade grave

> (3.3.65–70)

The list of swiftly terrible events and the reference to 'an unmade grave' carry the chill of prophecy, yet the use of these to justify 'fall[ing] upon the ground as I do now' is also a cartoon-like moment, in which Romeo is frozen in a ridiculous pose for the audience to take stock of him. (Both the posturing and the calling attention to it resemble the stance of Silvio, the absurdly lovesick shepherd of *As You Like It*, at 2.4.33–43.)

These comic shafts continue almost to the end of the play. The Nurse's fickle change of heart when it seems that the better course for Juliet would be to take Paris as her husband rather than try to oppose the tide is outrageously comic ('Romeo's a dishclout to him' (3.5.219)); and even at the point where Juliet is found seemingly dead, not only do the rhetorical excesses of the grief expressed by Paris and the Nurse seem to verge on the comic, but their outpouring of grief is immediately followed by a scene in which the musicians, having arrived to escort Juliet to church, are entreated by Peter to play 'some merry dump to comfort me' (4.5.105–6). The comic contradiction in Peter's words (a 'dump' is a sad tune), together with the total inappropriateness of his attempt to insist on the musicians playing, takes attention right away from the sorrow of the death scene. Juliet is of course not dead, which is one explanation for the placing of this scene. On the other hand, she will die; and this scene is one of many that falsely suggest a comic resolution to come.

Core scene: 1.5

Act 1, scene 5, is emblematic of the play in many ways, bringing together as it does this falsely reassuring comic dimension and the intensity of interaction that will in fact lead to its tragic outcome. A feast scene, as noted in chapter 1, is a recurrent motif in Shakespearean and other Elizabethan drama, not limited to either tragedy or comedy; but Capulet's feast includes a ball and is interrupted by a masque (or mask), both more usually comic motifs in Shakespeare. *Much Ado About Nothing* has a masked ball which provides the occasion for various different loves to be concealed, revealed and explored, while *The Merchant of Venice* uses a masque, a carnivalesque device that licenses free movement in disguise about the streets and into unfamiliar houses, to allow Lorenzo and Jessica, lovers similarly hemmed in by social prohibitions, to elope in disguise. The ball is not itself masked in *Romeo and Juliet*, though it is sometimes represented in that way (as in the Luhrmann film). Romeo and his friends hit on the idea of 'masking' as the excuse for their uninvited intrusion on the Capulet ball. Mercutio is masked, but Romeo, who chooses to be a torch-bearer rather than a full participant in the conceit of the mask, is probably unmasked, which is why Tybalt so easily recognises him. The scene begins as it would in a comedy, with servants moving busily about, Capulet joking about ladies prevented from dancing by their corns and a nostalgic conversation between Capulet and his cousin about their masking and dancing days. It is into this genial, colloquial and easy exchange that Romeo suddenly intrudes with lyrical intensity as he catches sight of Juliet:

> O, she doth teach the torches to burn bright.
> It seems she hangs upon the cheek of night
> As a rich jewel in an Ethiop's ear
> . . .
> Did my heart love till now? Forswear it, sight.
> For I ne'er saw true beauty till this night.
>
> (43–5, 51–2)

The change to rhyming couplets is made even more emphatic by the fact that the start and finish of this speech choose the same rhyming sound.

Tragedy again seems to be headed off as Tybalt recognises Romeo but is prevented from hostile action by the authoritative intervention of Capulet; and all at once Romeo is no longer talking about Juliet but directly to her, with astounding boldness, touching her and offering to kiss her before any other words have been exchanged. His words begin a sonnet, divided between the two of them in parallel units of almost equal length and almost equal frankness. If the speed of Romeo's move to touch and kiss is breathtaking, so too is the ease with which Juliet welcomes it, accepting the kiss with which the sonnet concludes. In this respect the encounter is totally unlike the encounter between Beatrice and Benedick in *Much Ado*, where desire, rather than confess itself too quickly, plays games and seeks to hide itself. Both the speed and the intensity of this moment initiate the sense of extremity leading directly towards the tragic outcome. The rush of love prompts both the lovers to thoughts of death:

> ROMEO
>   Is she a Capulet?
> O dear account. My life is my foe's debt.
>
>   (116–17)

> JULIET
>   Go ask his name. If he be married,
> My grave is like to be my wedding bed.
>
>   (133–4)

Love and death

From here the speed of events (condensed into a few days from several months in the source, Arthur Brooke's *Tragical History of Romeus and Juliet* (1562)), and the intensity of emotion combine with elements of chance to bring that expected end, and the choric utterances already noted concentrate on excess and the inevitability of death. The Chorus introducing Act 2 (which is also the last Chorus of the play) follows immediately on from the ball scene, linking time and passion together in the closing couplet (and linking back also to both the first Chorus and the first meeting between Romeo and Juliet by virtue of its sonnet form):

> But passion lends them power, time means, to meet,
> Tempering extremities with extreme sweet.
>
>   (13–14)

The Friar advises temperance and measure in vain:

> Therefore love moderately; long love doth so.
> Too swift arrives as tardy as too slow.
>
>   (2.6.14–15)

Juliet pronounces on the excessiveness of her own love:

> But my true love is grown to such excess
> I cannot sum up sum of half my wealth.
>
> (2.6.33–4)

Banishment is an extremity almost expected following the excess of love and anticipating the final unboundedness of death:

> There is no end, no limit, measure, bound,
> In that word's death. No words can that woe sound;
>
> (3.2.125–6)

Juliet anticipates her wedding night and her death bed as one and the same thing:

> Come, cords, come, Nurse, I'll to my wedding bed,
> And death, not Romeo take my maidenhead!
>
> (3.2.136–7)

and the Friar voices the same equation between marriage and death in relation to Romeo:

> Affliction is enamour'd of thy parts
> And thou art wedded to calamity.
>
> (3.3.2–3)

Even Juliet's own mother is made to express her anger at Juliet's stubborn refusal to marry Paris with an excess of violence that is both random (in realistic terms) and necessary (in terms of the play's increasingly insistent linking of extreme love with death): 'I would the fool were married to her grave' (3.5.140).

Romeo's 'Then I defy you, stars!' (5.1.24), if this is indeed what Shakespeare wrote, stands out as a lone attempt to oppose the coming of death against the much more frequent resignation inherent in the verbal text even as the actions of the Friar and the lovers struggle to take action against such an outcome.[3] The physical prominence of the tomb throughout Act 5 (verbally anticipated from the start of this play, and echoing its strong prominence throughout *Titus Andronicus*) gives monumental presence and seeming inevitability to the coming of death. As Michael Neill has noted in his illuminating study of early modern attitudes towards death, the tomb has reverberations of the older Christian drama dealing with resurrection, and can function as a symbol of either transience or transcendence.[4] Individual productions and their audiences will probably decide which is uppermost in the experience of *Romeo and Juliet*; but certainly the combination of the physical location with the fact that each of the lovers dies upon a kiss, seems to give physical form to an essential union between love and death enacted in this play. At the same time, however, chance occurrences, such as the way the Friar's letter misses Romeo, continually remind the audience that disaster could have been averted. Death is offered as both avoidable (as in comedy) and unavoidable, raising the question of whether death seems more tragic if it is presented as necessary. This will be a question to return to in Shakespeare's two later tragedies of love, *Othello* and *Antony and Cleopatra*. Meanwhile, in *Romeo and Juliet*, as in all Shakespeare's other tragedies, order must be restored in the state, and this is done very fully, with the reconciliation of Montague and Capulet. The love at least is seen to have had value, indeed power to change the world, though notably only through the deaths of the lovers. The generic mixture of the play lingers right to the end. Reconciliation, even when effected through death, has the stamp of comic closure about it.

Chapter 4

Julius Caesar

Julius Caesar may well have been the play Shakespeare wrote for the opening of the new Globe Theatre in 1599. It was very probably the play that Thomas Platter, a Swiss visitor to London, saw in September of that year, though the argument has recently been made that it inaugurated the new theatre in the previous June.[1]

> After dinner on 21 September, at about two o'clock, I went with my companions over the water and in the thatched-roof house saw the tragedy of the first Emperor Julius with at least fifteen characters very pleasingly acted. At the end of the comedy, they danced, according to their custom, exceedingly gracefully: two attired in men's clothes and two in women's performed wonderfully with one another.
>
> Thomas Platter, Observations on the Elizabethan Theatre (1599)

Platter's account functions as a useful reminder that plays at this time, including tragedies, were normally followed by the performance of a 'jig', often a bawdy, comic song-and-dance routine, though this particular post-show entertainment seems to have been a more formal dance. Though we no longer know what was staged after Shakespeare's other tragedies, we do well to remember that even the most awe-inspiring tragedy might have been followed by clowning and obscenity, a point which puts the mingled dramaturgy of the tragedies themselves into a culturally specific and now unfamiliar context. *Julius Caesar* is possibly one of the least dramaturgically mixed tragedies of Shakespeare's composition, containing as it does only one very brief comic interlude, in the first scene, but that is one of its defining features rather than part of Shakespeare's normal way of working.

Rome and republicanism

Shakespeare returns to Rome for the setting of *Julius Caesar*, but not the imperial Rome of *Titus Andronicus*. Here the focus is on the Roman republic, and the question on which the play turns is whether Caesar has ambitions to be a king, and thereby to end the republic. Political questions are much more continuously central to *Julius Caesar* than they are to *Titus Andronicus*, and both plot and character are almost entirely built around them. The politics of the Elizabethan succession were of course even more pressing in 1599 than they had been seven years earlier, when Shakespeare wrote *Titus*. There was greater unrest about Elizabeth's style of government and anxiety about the possibility of civil war in the absence of a clear succession. The Earl of Essex, whose return from Ireland may have been celebrated in *Henry V*, written very close in time to *Julius Caesar*, was to mount his rebellion against the Queen in 1601, using a performance of *Richard II* (probably Shakespeare's *Richard II*) to incite popular support, and Elizabeth was already highly sensitive to the publication of historical material that seemed to use history as a vehicle for criticising her own government. John Hayward's *The Life and Reign of King Henry IV*, treating the deposition and death of Richard II and opening with an extremely flattering dedication to Essex, was published in 1599. By summer of 1600 the book had been suppressed and burned and Hayward was imprisoned in the Tower.

men might safely write of others in manner of a tale; but in manner of a history, safely they could not: because, albeit they should write of men long since dead, and whose posterity is clean worn out; yet some alive, finding themselves foul in those vices which they see observed, reproved, and condemned in others, their guiltiness maketh them apt to conceive, that, whatsoever the words are, the finger pointeth only at them.

John Hayward, dedication to *Lives of the III Normans* (1613)

Shakespeare's Roman republic, though sufficiently distant from the Elizabethan state to avoid the fate of Hayward's history, still quite deliberately recalls Elizabethan London, with its 'walls and battlements', 'towers and windows' and 'chimney-tops' (1.1.39–40). The play's first scene, rejecting the ceremonial beginning of *Titus* and the formal chorus of *Romeo and Juliet*, opens *in medias res*, with the tribunes rebuking the commoners, who are celebrating Julius Caesar's triumphant return from victory over Pompey. The carpenter, reprimanded for failing to display the signs of his occupation, a leather apron and a rule, and the cobbler, quibbling with the tribunes over the nature of his occupation, are as English and Elizabethan as any workmen could be, and the strong sense of contemporary life that they exude gives a very different context to the political struggles that follow than would an attempt to fully Romanise them. (In representing the play's most serious concerns through lower class characters and comic dialogue, this opening scene resembles 1.1 of *Romeo and Juliet*.) The bringing of contemporary London into ancient Rome is deliberate;

it allows the fears that come in the train of a change of government to be experienced not just as historical and fictional fears, but as potential fears within the real and surrounding world of the audience. The keyword of the scene is its closing word: 'fearfulness' (1.1.76). David Farr's production of the play at Stratford in 2004 used short sharp bursts of communal nervous laughter throughout this opening scene to suggest a state of nervousness under a harsh regime; and the play endorses such a reading in the next scene, when it is revealed that the tribunes, 'for pulling scarves off Caesar's images, are put to silence' (1.2.284–5). The comedy of the opening scene never returns.

In dramatising *Julius Caesar* Shakespeare was drawing for the first time on a source that was to be central to four of his tragedies: Plutarch's *Lives of the Noble Grecians and Romans*, published in Sir Thomas North's translation in 1579. Plutarch, a Greek writer of the first century AD, was sympathetic to republicanism, a political position inherently challenging to the absolute monarchy of the Elizabethan state; but quite how sympathetic Shakespeare was to republicanism cannot be deduced from the play. David Daniell discusses in some detail the changes Shakespeare makes to Plutarch, showing his careful refusal to bias the play in one direction or another.[2] The political views represented in the play are always in dialogue, and Caesar's assassination is presented from conflicting perspectives, most notably by the funeral orations of Brutus and Mark Antony. Indeed rhetoric not only represents but also constructs political reality.

Shakespeare's presentation of the crowd veers from representing it through individuals like the carpenter and the cobbler, ordinary working men who can be performed either as knowing and witty citizens or as foolish, fickle clowns, to representing it as a single entity, 'the mob', easily manipulated, acting as one to destroy Cinna the poet merely because his name is the same as that of a conspirator (3.3), or seen through the lens of patrician hostility, as when Caska describes Caesar's refusal of the crown:

> and still as he refused it, the rabblement hooted, and clapped their
> chopped hands, and threw up their sweaty nightcaps, and uttered such
> a deal of stinking breath because Caesar refused the crown that it had
> almost choked Caesar; for he swooned and fell down at it. And for mine
> own part, I durst not laugh, for fear of opening my lips and receiving the
> bad air.   (1.2.242–9)

As the critical response to Deborah Warner's 2005 London production, with its hundred-strong crowd, showed, the strong presence of a really large crowd of actors, and the way they perform that presence, can swing the audience's response to the entire play.

What has often been celebrated as a supposed 'universality' in Shakespeare, free of time and place, is in fact an extreme openness and indeterminacy, which leaves the maximum flexibility for individual productions to inflect the plays according to the time and place of performance, making audiences feel that they are seeing something of direct relevance to them. The Roman plays, with their nuanced consideration of different forms of government, were especially frequently performed, for example, in Eastern European countries before the fall of the Berlin Wall.

Ethics, character and agency

The first half of the play is set broadly in and around the city; but the opening stage direction of 2.1, '*Enter Brutus in his orchard*', signals an important change of space, from the public to the private. (Despite the long-standing editorial practice of giving a location for every scene, Shakespeare only rarely scripts a location. When he does so, therefore, it is significant.) This is a notably public play, where characters are rarely seen in private. Julius Caesar himself, for example, is never seen completely alone. Even in the relative privacy of the next scene (2.2), where he enters in his nightgown and speaks with his wife, as Brutus does in 2.1, he is never alone and is visited by Decius as well as his wife and servant. Brutus, by contrast, is emphatically alone in 2.1, dismissing his servant; and it is here that the semblance of full interiority, that aspect of the tragic hero which has since come to seem naturalised as a defining feature of tragedy itself, is first developed. Brutus, as David Daniell suggests, both 'is, and is not, the tragic hero'.[3] He has the most lines in the play, but he is neither the titular hero, nor the single, central protagonist in a play which is very much an ensemble piece. The interiority Shakespeare constructs for him nevertheless goes beyond that of any tragic protagonist hitherto, with the arguable exception of Richard II, whose interiority is quite fully developed, though in a more lyrical vein.

But the defining context for the private is political. The main source for the development of Brutus' inner fullness lies in his ethical dilemma, and that dilemma itself hinges on a practical political question: how can the Roman republic be saved from a return to the absolute and potentially tyrannical rule of kings? Brutus is positioned by his own family history to respond with particular passion to the threat of tyranny, since his ancestor, Junius Brutus, led the revolt against the Tarquins which finally rid Rome of its monarchs. It is Cassius who first makes reference to that former Brutus who 'would have brooked / Th'eternal devil to keep his state in Rome / As easily as a king'

(1.2.158–60), but Brutus himself recalls him too in making his promise to Rome to strike for freedom (2.1.53–4). Caesar's ambition creates a collision between Brutus as an individual and Caesar's close friend, and Brutus as a citizen, passionately committed to a particular vision of Rome. The political choice (to save the republic) necessitates a moral choice (to kill Caesar), and it is the centrality of this moral question that makes character begin to seem so important.

Little in either *Titus Andronicus* or *Romeo and Juliet* prepares us for this kind of hero. Both Titus and Romeo are set at odds with the world that surrounds them, but neither Titus' drive towards revenge nor Romeo's towards love is constructed as an ethical dilemma or as primarily a psychological situation. Brutus is constructed from the start as divided from himself by the moral problematic of his situation. In response to Cassius' observation that Brutus no longer shows him 'that gentleness / And show of love as I was wont to have', Brutus begs him not to construe his neglect as anything other 'Than that poor Brutus, with himself at war, / Forgets the shows of love to other men' (1.2.33–4, 46–7). But, as Brutus' silence on the matter both with Cassius and with his wife indicates, his way of dealing with this is the Roman way of Stoicism. (The ethics of Stoicism, an ancient classical philosophy, were based on the principle that virtuous behaviour is purely rational, while the passions are essentially irrational.) He bears his suffering with silent fortitude. Where Romeo writhes on the ground and Titus goes mad when their sorrows become too much too bear, Brutus withdraws into himself. And this stoic endurance becomes the ground of manhood in *Julius Caesar* (a ground already implied by the friar's questioning of Romeo's manhood when he gives way to grief). Cassius' stories of Caesar's weak moments (1.2.100–31), added by Shakespeare to his source material, are designed to allow Cassius to suggest a Roman scorn for men who let their failings show, as opposed to remaining rigid exemplars of *virtus*, the kind of manhood defined by courage, nobility, honour and endurance. When Antony repeats that Brutus and his co-conspirators are 'honourable men' in his oration on Caesar (3.2.74–128) he is using a term especially resonant in Roman culture, which makes the note of irony all the more damaging. In his brief oration for Brutus after his death, however, he returns to these same terms of praise without irony: Brutus was 'the noblest Roman of them all'; of him, 'nature might stand up / And say to all the world, "This was a man!"' (5.5.75–6). There can be no higher praise within the world of this play.

It is partly because Brutus does not speak openly to others of his inner life that soliloquy becomes such an important vehicle for conveying his thoughts. Cynthia Marshall has argued that it is 'the encounter with Plutarch' that establishes 'our culture's prevailing model of character as one that is at once intensely performative and putatively interiorized' (and the performativity of character will be discussed more fully below); but as John Roe points out, '[n]othing in Plutarch's Life of Julius Caesar or of Marcus Brutus quite prepares us for those extended soliloquies with which Shakespeare equips Brutus'.[4] When we first encounter him in soliloquy he is in the closing stages of an internal debate, reaching the stark conclusion with which the speech opens, that the resolution of the dilemma facing Rome 'must be by his [Caesar's] death' (2.1.10). The speech is cool, rational, analytical, setting personal considerations on one side in favour of political issues. He decides to act on the basis that Caesar *may* become tyrannical because of his elevation, not that he shows any evident signs of becoming so: 'So Caesar may. / Then, lest he may, prevent' (2.1.27–8). The logic is carefully sequenced, but it is self-evidently not the only available logical sequence of thought in the circumstances.

In this interior world of abstract reason, violence is considered rather than passionate, calculated rather than excessive. Like Titus, Brutus tries to argue that he and his co-conspirators should be 'sacrificers but not butchers', 'purgers, not murderers' (2.1.165, 179); but the horror of the decision has its own life apart from these attempts to rationalise it, and Brutus' awareness of this is implied by the fact that he has to struggle to reconcile himself to it. Though his reasoning proceeds calmly, he also speaks of sleeplessness and inner turmoil in a way that foreshadows the more passionate and disturbed sufferings of Hamlet and Macbeth:

> I have not slept.
> Between the acting of a dreadful thing
> And the first motion, all the interim is
> Like a phantasma or a hideous dream:
> The genius and the mortal instruments.
>
> (2.1.62–6)

Part of his Stoicism is that he is able to carry through the assassination to the end, despite his inner recoil from it. James Mason, playing Brutus in Joseph Mankiewicz's 1953 film, misrepresents Shakespeare's Brutus by staggering back and away from Caesar before stabbing him. Such hesitation is only ever prior and inward in Shakespeare's Brutus; in the event he is a full participant, as a resolved man of honour must be.

One of the unresolved problems of the play, however, as elsewhere in Shakespeare's tragedies, is how to bring together this emphasis on human agency with the opposing emphasis on the superhuman: dreams, portents, ghosts, thunder and lightning. Before any of the conspirators has uttered an opinion on the question of Caesar's aspiration to sole power, the soothsayer is heard warning

Caesar to 'beware the Ides of March' (1.2.18). Later in that same scene, Cassius, following his exposure of Caesar's weakness to make the point that he is a mere man, not a God, acknowledges that he is nevertheless great, 'he doth bestride the narrow world / Like a colossus', and that such greatness is not a matter of fortune or fate but of personality:

> Men at some time are masters of their fates.
> The fault, dear Brutus, is not in our stars
> But in ourselves, that we are underlings.
>
> (1.2.134–5, 138–40)

But the next two consecutive scenes, including 2.1, in which we see Brutus and the conspirators reach agreement about how to proceed against Caesar, give substantial time to creating the special effects of a terrible storm and word-pictures of other outrageous breaches of nature, such as graves opening and a lioness whelping in the streets.

What kind of world is this, where men seem at the same time to be masters of their own fates and yet part of a world in which their acts are either foreseen or predestined? Are the gods so frequently mentioned in the play directing it towards particular outcomes or merely responding to what men do? This is a problem Shakespeare has already touched on briefly in the shaping of *Romeo and Juliet*, through both its Choruses and its references to Fortune. It is also one that Marlowe had addressed with particular force and equal uncertainty in a Christian context in *Dr Faustus*, where it is never clear how far the good and evil angels, traditional in the older drama, are external forces working on Faustus or externalisations of forces within him. Something similar might be said of the Ghost who appears to Brutus before Philippi. His status is openly questioned and answered:

> BRUTUS
> Art thou some god, some angel, or some devil,
> That mak'st my blood cold, and my hair to stare [stand on end]?
> Speak to me what thou art.
>
> GHOST
> Thy evil spirit, Brutus.   (4.3.277–80)

But exactly how clear does this leave us? Does Brutus' evil spirit come from inside or outside him? The question will recur, with different answers, in *Macbeth*. The comparison with North's Plutarch, which tells us that the appearance of the ghost 'showed plainly, that the gods were offended with the murder of Caesar' seems to show an evident and characteristic intent on

Shakespeare's part to leave the question more open.[5] Cassius, the most hard-headed realist in the play, offers the view that the gods work through human beings:

> Cassius from bondage will deliver Cassius.
> Therein, ye gods, ye make the weak most strong;
> Therein, ye gods, you tyrants do defeat;
>
> (1.3.90–2)

but it is far from clear that the play as a whole endorses Cassius' view. A similar uncertainty about where free will ends and the spirit world takes over will later dominate *Macbeth*.

Core scene: 2.1.232–308

In a play where public life and public appearance are so essential to the nature of the action, the scripting of a private encounter is likely to be highly significant. Brutus' conversation with his wife, Portia, in Act 2, scene 1, is a crucial moment in terms of what it tells us about Brutus, Rome and Roman ideals. It is Portia's only substantial appearance in the play and indeed one of only two moments in the play when women are at all significant. (The other is Calphurnia's appearance in the next scene to warn Caesar not to leave the house on a day when her dream has joined with other auguries to suggest terrible things to come.) There are conspicuous similarities between these two moments: both present women expressing urgent concern about their husbands in the early hours of the morning; both show men seemingly responsive to the pleading of their wives, but finally turning from them to the masculine world of business. Indeed the rest of the play, outside these two scenes, and unlike *Romeo and Juliet*, with its balancing of masculine and feminine, represents a very masculine world, strongly driven by male ideals of conduct. Virtue and manhood are inextricably bound up together, as Shakespeare would have known, in the Latin word *virtus* derived from Latin *vir*, a man. (As Plutarch expressed it, in North's translation, 'in those days, valiantness was honoured in Rome above all other virtues: which they called *virtus*, by the name of virtue itself, as including in that general name, all other special virtues besides'.)[6]

The extract under consideration here is closely modelled on a passage in Plutarch, but differs from it in important respects. Plutarch begins by telling the reader that because Portia 'would not ask her husband what he ailed before she had made some proof by her self . . . [she] took a little razor such as barbers occupy to pare men's nails, and . . gave herself a great gash withal in her thigh'.[7]

He goes on to give details of the 'vehement fever' that then took her and the extreme pain of the wound, and has her speak to Brutus 'even in her greatest pain'. Shakespeare proceeds very differently, showing the dialogue between Portia and Brutus first, before revealing the wound. In this exchange, each is concerned about the other, Brutus about Portia exposing herself to the cold night airs at this time and Portia about the change in Brutus' condition, which she knows to be due to some unspoken torment. When Brutus tries to dismiss her worries with assurances that he is simply unwell, Portia becomes both more insistent and more pleading, kneeling to Brutus to beg him to share the grief which 'by the right and virtue of my place / I ought to know of' (2.1.268–9)

This tableau of a woman kneeling to a man to whom she owes obedience is to be often repeated in the tragedies, with a range of different inflections. Lavinia kneels to her father for blessing on his return home, and the consequences of Tamora's kneeling in vain for mercy have been discussed in chapter 2 above. As these differing examples show, kneeling can represent female submissiveness, but it can also function to highlight a forced or unwilling adoption of submission. Here the kneeling is partly working to frame the challenging content of Portia's words within a physical posture which will proclaim her as a virtuous and obedient wife despite the strongly assertive mode of her speech. When Brutus urges her to 'Kneel not, gentle Portia', her reply is caustic: 'I should not need, if you were gentle Brutus' (277–8). To exclude her from his worries, she argues, in an image that takes the audience momentarily into the world of the London environment outside the theatre, is to keep her 'in the suburbs' of his pleasure, to treat her as his 'harlot, not his wife' (284–6). But as the discourse leads up to Portia revealing her wound it becomes more masculine as a consequence of becoming more Roman:

> I grant I am a woman: but withal
> A woman that Lord Brutus took to wife.
> I grant I am a woman: but withal
> A woman well reputed, Cato's daughter.
> Think you I am no stronger than my sex
> Being so fathered and so husbanded?
> Tell me your counsels. I will not disclose 'em.
> I have made strong proof of my constancy,
> Giving myself a voluntary wound,
> Here in the thigh. Can I bear that with patience,
> And not my husband's secrets?   (291–301)

Where in Plutarch the wound functioned to give Portia the right to ask her husband what is wrong, in *Julius Caesar* it becomes a weapon to challenge him with. As Coppélia Kahn has shown, it destabilises the gendered concept of virtue, as Portia imitates male constancy and enters the domain of warriors with a wound in this concealed and private part of her female body.[8] The scene points towards the tragedy to come by exposing the vulnerability at the heart of the *virtus* aspired to by all the male principals, but most rigorously, and inflexibly, embodied in Brutus.

Actor and role

Once we become aware of masculinity as under threat in this aggressively masculine world, it is possible to hear the ubiquitous self-assertion of its rival males as so much posturing. The play, dispersing its centre across several principals as opposed to focusing strongly on a single tragic hero, often gives them strongly competitive 'I am' statements. This is a rhetoric that Shakespeare first tries out in *Richard III*, creating an effect that mixes strong defiance with fear: 'Richard loves Richard, that is, I am I' (5.3.183). (As this quotation shows, it is closely linked to another rhetorical device prominent in the play known as 'illeism', excessive reference to oneself in the third person.) This insistent 'I am' is to reach its apogee in *Coriolanus*, but is a feature shared amongst the rival males of *Julius Caesar*. It is part of what makes Caesar seem both a Colossus and a performer of his greatness: 'always I am Caesar' (1.2.211); 'I am constant as the northern star' (3.1.60); and it becomes laughable when openly competitive, as in the quarrel between Brutus and Cassius:

CASSIUS
          I am a soldier, I,
Older in practice, abler than yourself
To make conditions.

BRUTUS
Go to, you are not, Cassius.

CASSIUS
          I am.

BRUTUS
I say you are not.   (4.3.30–4)

Antony, the greatest actor of them all, shows his skill in the way he performs his 'I am' with assumed but persuasive modesty:

I am no orator, as Brutus is,
But, as you know me all, a plain blunt man
That love my friend.   (3.2.210–12)

Ralph Fiennes' 'finest moment' as Antony in Deborah Warner's production, according to one reviewer, lay in his stumbling discovery of eloquence as a prop in the forum scene; but playing Antony in this way ignores the fact that he is scripted as a knowing performer before this point.[9] His meeting with the assassins immediately after Caesar's death, when he shakes each man by the hand, naming each as he does so, pausing to praise the corpse of the murdered Caesar in their presence, and showing the self-consciousness of that pause by making explicit reference to it (3.1.218–19), shows already the great actor who will take the people by storm in his funeral oration for Caesar.

The scene of Antony's triumph (3.2) is also notable for its scripting of stage-picture in a play that is otherwise very verbal and relatively static by comparison with the strongly pictorial *Titus*. Both Brutus and Antony go up into a pulpit (either a free-standing structure on stage or the gallery space above) to deliver their speeches, and Antony is scripted to enter with the body of Caesar, though it is not clear precisely how the body is borne. Joseph Mankiewicz seized on the potential of this to create the most memorable tableau of his film version, by having Marlon Brando appear with Caesar in his arms and stand still for a moment under the magnificent door at the top of the steps before descending to speak.

The play, by contrast, constructs a more cynical ongoing awareness of theatricality in a sequence of metatheatrical references. Caesar fears Cassio because 'He loves no plays / As thou dost, Antony; he hears no music' (1.2.202–3); Caska describes the mob clapping and hissing Caesar's refusal of the crown 'as they use to do the players in the theatre' (1.2.259); Brutus advises his fellow-conspirators to bear themselves on the day of the assassination 'as our Roman actors do, / With untired spirits and formal constancy' (2.1.223–6); and the sequence reaches a climax in the scene of the assassination itself, as the worldly Cassius instructs the conspirators to bathe their hands in Caesar's blood:

> Stoop, then, and wash. How many ages hence
> Shall this our lofty scene be acted over
> In states unborn and accents yet unknown?
>
> (3.1.111–13)

It is instructive to compare this strongly theatrical self-awareness with the kind of moment, already discussed in chapter 2, where a speaker pulls back from the story momentarily to see it as a story. Such moments have features in common with both metatheatricality and with choric or quasi-choric speech in *Romeo and Juliet*, but the implicit suggestion of posturing inherent in the metatheatrical utterances here is certainly not present in choric speech and is not routinely present in metanarrative utterance. We may test this by comparing the quotations above with the last moments of Brutus' life, when he constructs his death as the completion of the narrative that was his life:

> So fare you well at once, for Brutus' tongue
> Hath almost ended his life's history:
> Night hangs upon mine eyes; my bones would rest,
> That have but laboured to attain this hour.
>
> (5.5.39–42)

There is a summative quality about this utterance at the point of death that resists a reading of it as mere posturing, though it is not closed to the possibility of all negative reading.

How we understand Brutus at this moment is germane to the play's claim to tragic status. So too are the attitudes towards death expressed in the play. Caesar's pronouncement on death shortly before his own murder has the aura of self-aggrandising performance at first, but modulates into something more thoughtful:

> Cowards die many times before their deaths;
> The valiant never taste of death but once.
> Of all the wonders that I yet have heard,
> It seems to me most strange that men should fear,
> Seeing that death, a necessary end,
> Will come when it will come.   (2.2.32–7)

Reconcilement to death will become a recognisable attitude expressed by several of Shakespeare's later tragic heroes. Suicide, however, a hastening rather than a simple acceptance of death, is the end for several characters in the play: Portia, Cassius, Titinius and finally Brutus. Brutus has earlier expressed the view that this is a 'cowardly and vile' way out and argued instead for the virtue of 'patience / To stay the providence of some high powers / That govern us below' (5.1.103–7). He has already displayed such patience in bearing the news of Portia's death, explaining to Messala that 'With meditating that she must die once / I have the patience to endure it now' (4.3.189–90), and in promising to find more time to mourn Cassius (5.3.101–3). The scene in which he goes from friend to friend asking each of them to kill him is one that positions the audience rather uncertainly: they know that Brutus has scorned this way out, and they see the burden it places upon the man who has to drive the sword into Brutus' breast; yet the rhetoric of Brutus' own farewell speech and of Antony's praise plead for a recognition of his nobility.

As in the two preceding tragedies discussed, social order is restored and honourable burial is part of that restoration. Though Brutus has not been a true centre of the play, it seems to rest its final case for tragedy in the person of Brutus. Given the structure of the play, however, with its dispersal of interest across four male principals, the death of Caesar half-way through and the heavy sequence of deaths measuring out the pace of Act 5, the audience feels the tragedy of a whole society and its values bearing down on the fate of Brutus.

Chapter 5

Hamlet

Hamlet presents a complex textual situation. It exists in three versions, with the first quarto (1603) very different from and markedly shorter than the second quarto (1604–5) and Folio (1623) versions. It is also very hard to date because, besides the probability that Shakespeare revised his own work, there are references indicating that a play on this subject, now referred to as the *Ur-Hamlet* and no longer extant, pre-existed Shakespeare's play.[1] I here follow Q2, noting textual variation where it is important to the discussion. No play illustrates Shakespeare's characteristically mixed dramaturgy or his dialogue with the popular theatre of his immediate predecessors better than *Hamlet*, which creates a hero with an ethical dilemma, like Brutus, and puts him in dialogue with the popular form of revenge tragedy.

The Chamberlain's Men, who performed *Hamlet* at the Globe, probably in 1600–1, were one of two companies who had dominated the London theatre scene since 1594. Theatre had by this time become truly embedded in London life, and the companies could make references to their previous plays or to the other company's plays in the expectation that audiences would understand the in-jokes and appreciate the flattery of being positioned so knowingly. Thus when Polonius tells Hamlet 'I did enact Julius Caesar. I was killed i' th' Capitol. Brutus killed me' (3.2.99–100), it is likely that the same actors who played Caesar and Brutus in *Julius Caesar* were again playing opposite each other here as Polonius and Hamlet. There is even a long and highly topical passage, existing only in the Folio text, where Hamlet inveighs against the child actors who 'are now the fashion' and widely applauded (2.2.335–60).[2] Confident, witty and innovative in the face of competition, Shakespeare and the Chamberlain's Men address a regular audience in *Hamlet* through a mixture of clowning and seriousness. Here the tragic hero is not separate from the clowns but rather separate to a degree from the court and capable himself of clowning and acting a role as well as of unpacking his heart. When he first appears, in 1.2, his black costume sets him apart, the Q2 stage direction scripts his entry last, out of rank order, and his characteristic mode of interaction with the King and Queen is through wordplay.[3]

Revenge

It is a truism of *Hamlet* criticism to say that the play examines the non-fit between the hero and the task of revenge. What I want to do here is look a little more closely at how that sense of non-fit is established in terms of reference to, and resistance to, the dramaturgical shapes of *Titus Andronicus* and *The Spanish Tragedy*. Conspicuously, the play opens quite differently from either, not with spectacle or ceremony, not with a scenic form that revels openly in the formal pleasures of the stage, but with an even more developed attempt than in *Julius Caesar* to simulate a real world and enter it *in medias res*. Two nervy sentinels meet on the battlements of Elsinore in a naturalistic dialogue that barely betrays its incipient blank verse form:

> BARNARDO
> Who's there?
>
> FRANCISCO
> Nay, answer me. Stand and unfold yourself.
>
> BARNARDO
> Long live the King!
>
> FRANCISCO
>   Barnardo.
>
> BARNARDO
>   He.
>
> FRANCISCO
> You come most carefully upon your hour.
> $(1.1.1-4)^4$

It is thus something of a surprise when the next conversation, following the entry of Horatio and Marcellus, reveals that the source of this anxiety is a ghost, which has appeared on the last two nights; and it is even more surprising when the ghost suddenly appears, disrupting their conversation. It is as though two worlds collide, not just in the obvious, narrative sense of the collision between the human world and the spirit world, but in the theatrical sense of a collision between two modes of dramaturgy, one dealing in verisimilitude and the other in high spectacle. There is a vast difference between Revenge and the Ghost of Andrea in *The Spanish Tragedy* appearing directly to the audience in a theatrical space that does not seek to represent anything in the known world and a ghost appearing in what is represented in *Hamlet* as real time and real space, refusing to speak.

At this point, then, before the need for revenge is made explicit, the play signals a relationship with that earlier play which opened with a ghost requiring revenge, but maintains a distance from it, a distance which widens during the Ghost's encounter with Hamlet. At first that gap seems to narrow and bring the play closer to *The Spanish Tragedy* as the Ghost's discourse moves into the high rhetoric of a long monologue describing the horror of the murder that needs to be avenged, but it then opens up with outrageous speed following the Ghost's disappearance from sight. Hamlet's speech at this point is remarkable. Rhetorical apostrophes ('O all you host of heaven, O earth') are undercut almost immediately by a theatrical in-joke as Hamlet vows to remember what the Ghost has said 'whiles memory holds a seat / In this distracted globe' (1.5.92, 96–7). The reference is simultaneously to the state of mind the performer is enacting and the theatre in which he is doing so, and it is a deeply unsettling moment, deliberately precluding the possibility of a sole focus on Hamlet's inner turmoil. As the speech continues, it multiplies difficulties for an audience waiting for modes of engagement familiar from a highly popular form. Instead of a rhetoric that aestheticises and ritualises the violence it sees and plans, the audience gets inchoate ranting and inexplicable behaviour: 'O villain, villain, smiling damned villain' (106). Hamlet raves; and then suddenly decides that this insight needs to be written down: 'Meet it is I set it down / That one may smile, and smile and be a villain' (107–8). The eccentricity of getting out writing materials at this point can scarcely be overstated. And in terms of reference to memorable moments from earlier revenge tragedy, what it seems to do is both recall and belittle the fetishised writing of those earlier plays, both the moment when Hieronimo finds the letter written in Bel-imperia's blood commanding him to revenge and giving him the names of his son's killers (*Spanish Tragedy*, 3.2) and the moment when Lavinia, deprived of hands and tongue, guides a stick in the sand with her stumps to write the words that will reveal the crime against her and those responsible (*Titus Andronicus*, 4.1).

The ritual swearing of the vow to revenge, so prominent in *Titus*, is next explicitly evoked and parodied as Hamlet, whom we might expect to pledge himself to revenge at this moment, instead merely swears his friends to secrecy with awkward insistence on making a ritual within a scene where the other characters are portrayed realistically enough to be merely embarrassed by the sudden shift to ritual. Even more outrageously, the Ghost is then made to join in from beneath the stage with a cry of 'Swear', and again Hamlet's response is to engage in emphatically naturalistic dialogue with the Ghost: 'Ha, ha, boy, sayst thou so? Art thou there, truepenny?', and to turn back to his friends with a casual insistence that simultaneously reminds the audience that the command to swear came not from a ghost beneath the earth but from an actor under the stage, a 'fellow in the cellarage' (1.5.149–51). Nothing could better measure the distance between *The Spanish Tragedy* and *Hamlet* than the fact that one play's terrible and terrifying presence becomes another play's comic moment of self-awareness. And Hamlet's crazed laughter here in the first act travesties the laughter Titus finally reaches when he can weep no more following the horrors of 3.1, just as Hamlet's feigning of an 'antic disposition' (1.5.170) seems to undercut the seriousness of the madness induced in both Titus and Hieronimo by grief.

Like *The Spanish Tragedy*, *Hamlet* has a play within a play, but, just as the ritual swearing in *Hamlet* is not to revenge but to mere secrecy, and not by the revenger but by his friends, so there is an obliqueness about the inserted play. It does not offer a ritual shape for the final acts of revenge, but instead merely tests the guilt of the murderer already identified as such by the ghost. Where the ghosts of the dead are sacred presences in *The Spanish Tragedy* and *Titus Andronicus*, shadows that must be appeased by ritual sacrifice, in *Hamlet* the Ghost's status is in doubt and his commands to revenge must be tested against hard evidence in the material world. When Hamlet plays up the revenger's passion, as when he claims he could 'drink hot blood' (3.2.380) or thrusts his sword through the arras in his mother's chamber, the contrast with the modes of being that we see him adopt elsewhere in the play constructs the sense that these moments are role-playing, verging on parody. Indeed the change in speech even within the same scene from 'How now! A rat!' through 'For this same lord / I do repent' to 'I'll lug the guts into the neighbour room' (3.4.22, 170–1, 210), deliberately sets up incompatible registers, comparable indeed with the contrast between Hamlet's occasional inchoate raving and his claim to be 'but mad in craft' (3.4.186).

The deaths themselves, when they finally occur, are not framed in the ritual of a masque but arise out of a sequence of unlucky accidents. These accidents are signalled well before Act 5 with events that ape Hamlet's promised revenge: his refusal to murder Claudius at prayer or his mistaken killing of Polonius, for example. The final scene seems at first to recognise the need for ritual shape: as in *Titus*, the table is set for a feast, and the fencing match seems to offer a formalised show analogous to masque. It begins ceremonially enough, with a processional entry, weapons brought in on cushions and the King placing Laertes' hand in Hamlet's. From there, however, ceremony and planning degenerate into a haphazard sequence: Gertrude drinks from the poisoned cup intended for Hamlet; Laertes wounds Hamlet, but '*in scuffling*', as the Folio stage direction puts it (5.2.285); the foils are exchanged and Hamlet wounds Laertes; and when Laertes then tells Hamlet that he is holding a poisoned foil, Hamlet uses it to kill Claudius. But none of these deaths except Hamlet's own was part of the plan for this fencing match; and the plans that were in place were, significantly, not the revenger's own, but those of his opponents.

Core scene: 5.1

In order to demonstrate the kind of mixed play that *Hamlet* is as well as some of its core elements, this section will proceed differently from earlier chapter analyses of core scenes, taking a long and important scene for analysis rather than a short and more self-contained extract and looking at the structural layering of moments as well as the moments themselves. Shakespeare's ongoing experimentation with tragic form is conspicuous in this long and complex scene, as it is in the loose and mingled structure of the play as a whole. Before looking at its opening, we need to be aware of how the previous scene (4.7) has ended: with Laertes' urgent desire for revenge on Hamlet, hearing of his father's death at Hamlet's hands; with Gertrude's lyrical description of Ophelia's death by drowning; and with the reinflammation of Laertes' rage that this news provokes. When 5.1 opens with two gravediggers digging Ophelia's grave and discussing whether Christian burial is appropriate for one whose death may have been suicide (a sin that debarred the sinner from Christian burial except in circumstances of mental imbalance),[5] a completely different perspective is cast on Ophelia's death from the responses of either Gertrude or Laertes, who do not voice the possibility of suicide. Indeed 5.1 is, amongst other things, a sequence of different perspectives on death prior to the final deaths of the tragedy. The precise logic of the first clown is comic, as are his jokes about gentlemen, gallows-makers and gravediggers, but there is a serious undertow making an important point about social class: that Ophelia would not have received Christian burial had she not been of gentle birth. Thus, against the inherent background of death the leveller (the idea that all human beings, whatever their class, come to the same thing in the end) is the fact that even after death distinctions are made that rank one human being above another.

Left alone, the first clown sings as he digs, and this is the cue for Hamlet and Horatio to enter. As Hamlet expresses shock at such lack of feeling, the gravedigger sings of how death comes to all, young and old alike. As Hamlet watches, the gravedigger carelessly throws up a skull and Hamlet is provoked to imagine the living individual who now is come to this. He speaks to Horatio, and their careful prose contrasts with the rhyming song of the clown until Hamlet directly addresses the clown, encountering, to his surprise, a precision more logical than his own. The very strategy of putting Hamlet in dialogue

with a clown marks a move from Shakespeare's earlier tragedy, which has little
to compare with this direct encounter across the boundaries of class, in which
the clown's strict logic gets the better of Hamlet.[6] In responding to Hamlet's
question as to how long he has been a gravemaker, he is even given a joke that is
(unwittingly from the character's point of view) targeted against both Hamlet
and the audience:

> GRAVE-DIGGER
> It was that very day that young Hamlet was born – he that is mad and
> sent into England.
>
> HAMLET
> Ay, marry. Why was he sent into England?
>
> GRAVE-DIGGER
> Why, because 'a was mad. 'A shall recover his wits there. Or, if 'a do not,
> 'tis no great matter there.
>
> HAMLET
> Why?
>
> GRAVE-DIGGER
> 'Twill not be seen in him there. There the men are as mad as he.
>
> (5.1.139–46)

The joke is not merely that the gravedigger is unknowingly addressing Hamlet
but that the audience is being teased with a joke about Englishmen. Thus,
though Hamlet's madness and Ophelia's death are highly serious matters within
the world of the play, the audience is made to step outside its serious engagement
with those matters in order to recognise and laugh at a joke on themselves. Part
of the serious point, furthermore, is that this version of Hamlet whom we now
see in the graveyard is very far from mad. Absent from the play throughout Act 4,
while he is in England, he returns to Denmark and the stage a different man. This
Hamlet, joking with the gravedigger and making serious observations about
life and death, is self-evidently sane at this moment, though his behaviour is
to change more than once in the course of the scene.

The perspective on death changes to the physical, as Hamlet asks how long
a corpse will take to rot, and this is a perspective reminiscent of the mystery
plays, still performed in some parts of England until 1579, in which the figure
of Lazarus commonly spoke at length of the horrors of the grave.[7] Thus the
play recalls an older tradition of Christian drama, combining the fear of death
with the hope of resurrection, at the same time as it moves towards a new
secularism, as the gravedigger hands Hamlet a skull that turns out to be personally meaningful to him. The image of Hamlet holding Yorick's skull is one

of the most famous emblematic moments in early modern theatre, perhaps in all western theatre, and the iconicity of the play is well brought out in Olivier's film version of 1948.[8] But it is a moment that faces in contradictory directions. The lament for the past ('Where be your jibes now – your gambols, your songs, your flashes of merriment, that were wont to set the table on a roar?' (179–81)) looks back to a classical tradition of lament, known by its Latin name as '*ubi sunt*' (where are . . .?). The Christian consolation is both summoned into view by the parallel with mystery plays and deliberately withheld. The disquisition on Alexander returning to dust (192–201) is strongly evocative of the 'dust to dust' wording of the Christian burial service, but turns instead into a bitter and cynical little rhyme that refuses the consolation evoked:

> Imperious Caesar, dead and turned to clay,
> Might stop a hole to keep the wind away.
> O, that that earth which kept the world in awe
> Should patch a wall t'expel the water's flaw.
>
> (206–9)

It is at this point that Ophelia's funeral procession enters, with Hamlet still unaware that the corpse is Ophelia's. Prose and rhyming jingle give way to verse and a marked change of tone, as Laertes tries to insist on the fuller rites that Ophelia would have if her death were not a suspected suicide. The lyrical tone of Gertrude's account of Ophelia's drowning returns briefly as she and Laertes scatter flowers on the grave, but is abruptly cut off by melodramatic gestures and high rhetoric that seem to belong to a different kind of play altogether. Where Hamlet's bitter knowningness about death seemed to signal the beginnings of secular modernity, now first Laertes, then Hamlet, leap into the grave, competing in their 'phrase of sorrow' (244) and physically attacking one another. Hamlet's high-sounding citation of his own name ('This is I, / Hamlet the Dane' (246–7)) has echoes of an earlier, bombastic dramatic tradition as well as of the masculine competitiveness of *Julius Caesar*, and strikes an attitude so far at odds with that adopted towards Horatio and the gravedigger as to suggest that it is precisely that: the striking of an attitude. The rhetoric becomes ranting, and both the King and Queen again think Hamlet mad. Hamlet's exit lines adopt a cryptic mode different again from the wit, the meditativeness, the bitterness or the raving that have gone before: 'Let Hercules himself do what he may, / The cat will mew and dog will have his day' (280–1); and the final lines of the scene are the King's as he plans ahead. The audience is equipped for viewing the last scenes of the play with a plurality of competing perspectives on death and a bewildering multiplicity of dramatic modes of engagement.

Acting and being

One way in which this plurality of perspectives and modes of engagement may be experienced is as a sequence of parts played by Hamlet. Indeed the question so often asked: 'Is Hamlet mad?' is a question arising out of an uncertainty as to when Hamlet is being 'himself' and when he is playing a part, and how an audience can know the difference. What the audience does know from the start is that Hamlet is preoccupied with the gap between what is visible to the outside world, the 'actions that a man might play', and 'that within which passes show' (1.2.84–5). The position of such a character is paradoxical, since the audience has to move between awareness of the actor as character and the character as actor. The sum of Hamlet's part consists of trying out or refusing the range of parts available to him. From his first entrance, swathed in black, standing apart, speaking in riddles, partly to the other characters, partly to the audience and partly to himself, it is evident that he does not 'belong' to the world of the play in the way that other characters do. In early modern performance, as Robert Weimann has shown, this blurred status, half-inside and half-outside the fiction, would have been made visible through Hamlet's tendency to occupy the outside edge of the stage, the liminal space between the world of the audience and the world of the play.[9]

Hamlet's semi-occupancy of the playworld is tied up with his task as a revenger, and this is what makes *Hamlet* a play which is ultimately a dialogue with the revenge play rather than a straightforward revenge play itself. In putting at the centre of this play a figure called upon to revenge but unable fully to *be* whatever part he plays, Shakespeare takes his experimentation with tragic form to new levels. In effect, what this play explores, moving on from the genre of revenge tragedy already explored in *Titus Andronicus*, is whether there is something more essentially tragic to be encountered in the condition of failing to revenge than in fulfilling it. For Hamlet there is a necessary division between doing and being and a resistance to being defined by the act. He is even instructed by the Ghost to keep his action separate from his being and to avoid allowing his mind to become tainted by the deed:

> But howsomever thou pursuest this act
> Taint not thy mind nor let thy soul contrive
> Against thy mother aught.   (1.5.84–6)

Being and not being, on which Hamlet's mind plays in his most famous soliloquy, is not just a matter of being alive or ceasing to be, but of thinking or doing, which should ideally be aligned and undivided and are not. Revenge is a part that Hamlet feels a duty to take on but cannot adapt to his being. He is shamed, ironically and necessarily, by a player whose performed weeping seems to have more force than his own inaction:

> What's Hecuba to him, or he to her,
> That he should weep for her? What would he do
> Had he the motive and the cue for passion
> That I have?   (2.2.494–7)

Both Hamlet and the play as a whole are obsessed by the idea of performance. Polonius' reminiscing about playing the part of Julius Caesar is emblematic, not accidental. Besides Hamlet's own running commentary on his actions as a set of performances, the play not only keeps inserting further plays into the play (the actor's speech that shames Hamlet; the dumb-show that precedes *The Mousetrap*; *The Mousetrap* itself, set up to shame Claudius and including an extra speech penned by Hamlet) but also has Hamlet instruct the players at length on how to act (3.2.1–42). And other scenes not explicitly set up as metatheatre in fact operate in that way. Thus, for example, Polonius, like a director instructing an actor, tells Ophelia to walk in a certain place and to appear to read a book so that he and the King can observe Hamlet in conversation with her, and Hamlet's famous 'To be or not to be' soliloquy thereby becomes a performance staged before an audience inside as well as outside the play (3.1). Even in Gertrude's closet, the most seemingly private space in this much spied-upon court, Polonius becomes a hidden audience to Hamlet's conversation with his mother, thus provoking his own death. Film is a particularly good medium for highlighting this specular and voyeuristic element in the play. Almereyda's 2002 film, for example, showed how viewing frames everything that happens in the play by incorporating images of photography, home videos, closed-circuit TV and multiple reflective surfaces, while Branagh (1996) used a circling camera to frame key moments in the two scenes above.

It is not coincidental that these two scenes are central to the way the women of the play are represented, as men's puppets. Ophelia is directed and constrained by Polonius, Gertrude allows both Claudius and Polonius to direct her, and both women are observed and despised by Hamlet, constructed by him as representative of womankind in general. While Hamlet is disgusted by his own inability to act the appointed part of revenger, he is even more disgusted by what he sees as a gendered willingness amongst women to put on a face and to betray whatever vows of loyalty they may have sworn by adopting new personae as necessary. His mother's brief performance of mourning, 'Like Niobe, all tears' (1.2.149), seems to him emblematic of the frailty that is woman, and Ophelia (who is indeed performing in some sense before the concealed audience of her father and the King in 3.1) becomes the focus of his same generalised bitterness against woman: 'I have heard of your paintings well enough. God has given you one face, and you make yourselves another' (3.1.141–3).

One reason why women within the world of this play can never be anything but actors is that *Hamlet*, unlike *Julius Caesar*, is so far from being an ensemble piece. On the contrary, Hamlet is the most isolated and singular of all Shakespeare's tragic heroes except Coriolanus, absorbing into himself all the play's introspective energy, all the angst that comes from a division between being and acting, and making most of the other characters look shallow by comparison. But this reductivism impacts more on the female than the male population of the play, since neither of the only two female characters is ever scripted to speak alone or directly to the audience. Even Claudius, a much more deliberate deceiver and actor than either Gertrude or Ophelia, with a real crime to hide, has his moment of interiority, when he reflects on his offence and tries to pray (3.3); but there is no indication that Gertrude has given any thought to her offence until Hamlet represents it to her as hideous (3.4). Ophelia's inner turmoil appears only in her madness, but that madness not only lacks the complexity of Hamlet's quasi-madness, it also aestheticises and reifies Ophelia.[10]

Claudius, himself far guiltier than any woman in the play, uses the image of the harlot as a metaphor for his own degradation:

> The harlot's cheek beautied with plastering art
> Is not more ugly to the thing that helps it
> Than is my deed to my most painted word;
>
> (3.1.50–2)

and Hamlet also compares himself to a whore, though for a different reason: because he is driven to 'unpack [his] heart with words' (2.2.520). Even in a play where women's input, both verbal and practical, is so restricted, the stereotype of the female chatterbox is brought in, allowing Hamlet to see his own own tendency to express himself more through words than through actions as calling his masculinity into question. If Ophelia's passivity is the product of her gender (as represented in this play), Hamlet's failure to act turns him against himself in a way that is parallel with his turn against women.

Doubt and resolution

What drives Hamlet to unpack his heart is doubt; and this makes the play very poignantly expressive of its historical moment, though it is also, paradoxically, what has enabled the play to speak so powerfully to other times and places.

Doubt, of course, can be interpreted by later generations and different cultures in a number of ways: as religious scepticism, as political resistance or as an existentialist commentary on the nature of being. But England in 1600 was reeling from a century of religious upheaval, as yet unresolved. Martin Luther had legendarily nailed his beliefs to the door of the Castle Church in Wittenberg in 1517 (and it is no accident that Hamlet and Horatio are established at the start of the play as students at the University of Wittenberg, nor that Hamlet is keen to return there to escape the Danish court); and Tyndale's English Bible, printed abroad, had been seized and burnt in London in 1525. Henry VIII's break with the church of Rome in 1534 began a sequence of huge swings in the religious policy of the state; and though the Elizabethan church settlement had held sway for some forty years by the end of the century, legislation still forbade plays to deal with religious subjects, and matters of religion were still burning issues for which some were prepared to die.

The Ghost is indeed a dubious figure, and Hamlet's doubts about whether to trust its commands cannot be dismissed as mere prevarication. Its opening words, anticipating the need to return to 'sulphurous and tormenting flames' (1.5.3), recalled to an Elizabethan audience the world of an older faith, cherishing the belief that the souls of the dead had to suffer in purgatory before they could be saved; yet the play does not explicitly endorse or advocate such a faith. On the contrary, it consciously puts opposing ideas into play, particularly in the last act, as Hamlet seems to reach a new calm based on a growing trust in providence: 'There's a divinity that shapes our ends, / Rough-hew them how we will'; 'There is special providence in the fall of a sparrow' (5.2.10–11, 197–8). Such faith in providence was central to Calvinist doctrine, and Calvin himself used the same example of the sparrow from the New Testament (Matthew 10.29) to insist upon it.[11] Reconcilement to death, however, is no purely partisan matter. It also has a Stoic aspect which predates all varieties of Christian faith, as discussed in chapter 4 above, and above all it offers a way of resolving the doubts and hesitations that have beset the play, of bringing the audience to a sense of acceptance of the tragedy. (Despite the precise bearing of this passage on a very specific cultural moment, twentieth-century performances of *Hamlet* have often focused on it as a moment of insight.)[12]

It is the beginning of the gradual restoration of order which routinely brings the tragedies to a close. Thus Fortinbras, who functions earlier in the play as a contrast and a potential rebuke to Hamlet, is made an acceptable successor to the throne of Denmark by having Hamlet's 'dying voice' (5.2.340) to his election; and Hamlet himself makes his final peace with the world by seeking to impose the restoration of order through narrative closure. 'Absent thee from felicity awhile', he begs Horatio, 'And in this harsh world draw thy breath in pain /

To tell my story' (5.2.331–3). This shaping of closure through a withdrawal from the story that allows the audience to see it *as* story is reminiscent not only of Brutus' end in *Julius Caesar*, but also of the Ghost's demand in this play to be remembered. But where the Ghost's demand to be remembered was inseparable from a demand to be revenged, Hamlet's request seeks to close rather than perpetuate acts of violence. This last act of remembrance is the acceptable face of the moral dilemma that has shaped the play.

Chapter 6

Othello

Othello was probably first performed soon after King James VI of Scotland acceded to the English throne in 1603.[1] James' accession meant a change in status for the Chamberlain's Men, who now became the King's Men, thereby acknowledged as the premier acting company in the country. Shakespeare's company performed on all the notable dates of the Christmas season 1603, by contrast with the previous year, when the dates were shared out fairly evenly between the companies.[2] Othello was performed at court, at the Whitehall Banqueting House, on 1 November 1604. Like most of Shakespeare's plays, however, it was also performed in the public theatre in London and probably taken on tour. An eyewitness account of a performance at Oxford University in 1610 survives, giving us a brief and fascinating window into one contemporary response to the play.

> In the last few days the King's players have been here. They acted with enormous applause to full houses . . . They had tragedies too which they acted with skill and decorum and in which some things, both speech and action, brought forth tears.
> Moreover, that famous Desdemona killed before us by her husband, although she always acted her whole part supremely well, yet when she was killed she was even more moving, for when she fell back upon the bed she implored the pity of the spectators by her very face.
> Letter by Henry Jackson, September 1610 (translated from the Latin)

Clearly pity, classified by Aristotle, with fear, as one of the two emotions that tragedy should evoke (p. 2 above), is a central part of this spectator's response, and it is the actor's face, not the grander spectacle suggested by the surviving sketch and contemporary response to Titus Andronicus, that is indicated as prompting that response. A boy-actor here immerses a spectator in the role he plays, as opposed to impressing him with an awareness of the play as a performance. The quieter key of this kind of acting suggests something of the road travelled by both Shakespearean tragedy and the King's Men's performance style over the decade between Titus and Othello. Though Othello contains high rhetoric and epic performance style, it is also a remarkably private and domestic tragedy. Othello serves the state of Venice, but the state barely impinges upon the tragedy at all. Unlike Hamlet, whose personal torment is inextricably tied up with the question of who rules Denmark, Othello suffers in ways that are almost sealed off from the surrounding political context of relations between Venice and Cyprus.

Black and white

Although the events that lead directly to the tragedy are largely segregated from the political events depicted in the play, however, the story of Othello's jealousy is in another way deeply imbued with the surrounding politics in the much broader sense that Othello is racially an outsider to the Venetian state. We hear of him before we see him on stage, as the play opens with Iago and Roderigo in conversation about him. We first learn of his race through a sneering reference by Iago to 'his Moorship' (1.1.32); and the implicit hostility of this is taken a step further by Roderigo's reference to him as 'the thicklips' (1.1.65). This is a discourse reminiscent of *Titus Andronicus*, which casts the villain, Aaron, as a black man and allows Marcus to justify his killing of the fly on the grounds that it was black, 'Like to the empress' Moor'. *Othello*, unlike *Titus*, will script a black man as the tragic hero; yet before this opening out of sympathy takes place Shakespeare not only makes a point of representing racial prejudice against Othello, but in particular makes Iago reiterate expressions of disgust for his marriage with a white woman:

> an old black ram
> Is tupping your white ewe;
>
> (1.1.87–8)

> your daughter covered with a Barbary horse;
>
> (1.1.110)

> your daughter and the Moor are now making the beast with two backs.
>
> (1.1.114–15)

We are made to understand that, while Othello's service in arms may be welcome to the state of Venice, he is not a welcome son-in-law for a Venetian senator. He can never truly become a Venetian. Productions of *Othello* which seem to have been most successful in the past are those which have conveyed his alienness in that environment most fully. Tommaso Salvini, who played Othello in Italian to English audiences in the nineteenth century, sometimes alongside fellow-actors speaking in English, seemed 'a barbarian, whose instincts, savage and passionate, are concealed behind a veneer of civilisation so thick that he is himself scarcely conscious he can be other than he appears'; while Willard White, a black opera singer unused to playing Shakespeare, seemed '[i]n a curious, almost disturbing way' to 'fit the role rather aptly, the alien among the Venetians, the black opera singer among the white Shakespeareans'.[3] Ian McKellen's very tactile Iago, playing against Willard White in Trevor Nunn's 1989 production, touched everyone except Othello.[4]

The black/white binary is reiterated throughout the play in a variety of ways, often aligning race with morality and with an angel/devil binary. Thus the Duke of Venice assures Desdemona's father of Othello's virtue in these terms:

> If virtue no delighted beauty lack
> Your son-in-law is far more fair than black;
>   (1.3.290–1)

and Othello himself comes close to making an equation between race and bad behaviour when he rebukes his men for brawling: 'Are we turned Turks?' (2.3.166). Indeed Othello moves, disturbingly, from trusting in Desdemona's love, to fearing that his race is the reason she has betrayed him ('Haply, for I am black . . .' (3.3.267)), to a finally abject parallel between his own blackness and Desdemona's supposed wickedness:

> Her name, that was as fresh
> As Dian's visage, is now begrimed and black
> As mine own face.   (3.3.389–91)

He comes to believe in Desdemona's breaking of faith, this parallel suggests, because he is already half-way to absorbing the negative view of his own worth that white Venetians offer him.

The engineer of this transformation, of course, is Iago, whose self-stated object is quite simply to blacken white and who speaks of himself in binary terms as a devil masked as an angel:

> When devils will the blackest sins put on
> They do suggest at first with heavenly shows
> As I do now.
> . . .
> So will I turn her virtue into pitch
> And out of her own goodness make the net
> That shall enmesh them all.
>   (2.3.346–8, 355–7)

Iago is a pure villain in a direct line of descent from Aaron the Moor, but in this play Shakespeare consciously reverses the skin alignment to make the hero black and the villain white. Like Aaron (and Richard III), Iago speaks boldly, frankly and sometimes wittily. It is he rather than Othello who takes on Hamlet's knowing and witty confidentiality with the audience. His sexual banter when Desdemona arrives in Cyprus moves into particularly risky territory when they talk about 'black' (that is, dark-haired) women, and the exchange seems to glance in reverse at the marriage Desdemona has just made:

> DESDEMONA
> How if she be black and witty?
>
> IAGO
> If she be black, and thereto have a wit,
> She'll find a white that shall her blackness fit.
> (2.1.131–3)

Against the strong 'I am' of tragic heroes, Iago pits a stronger force of self-knowledge and strength of will:

> I am not what I am;   (1.1.64)

> Virtue? a fig! 'tis in ourselves that we are thus, or thus. Our bodies are gardens, to the which our wills are gardeners.   (1.3.320–2)

And against Othello's increasingly desperate need to know ('If thou dost love me, / Show me thy thought' (3.3.118–19); 'By heaven, I'll know thy thoughts!' (3.3.164)) he pits his own ultimate unknowability:

> You cannot, if my heart were in your hand;
> (3.3.165)

> Demand me nothing. What you know, you know.
> From this time forth I never will speak word.
> (5.2.300–1)

The blackness of the play is also a darkness. At its centre is the fear of what is hidden, the fear that inside or underneath every fair appearance there is something monstrous and barbaric; or, as the dialogue between Othello and Iago constructs it:

> OTHELLO
> I am bound to thee for ever;
> (3.3.217)
>
> . . .
>
> IAGO
> I am your own for ever.
> (3.3.481)

Othello's skin colour, despite his evident nobility within, becomes emblematic in the play of the base desires that betray men and women.

The handkerchief

Thomas Rymer's contemptuous view of *Othello* is notorious.

> So much ado, so much stress, so much passion and repetition about an handkerchief! Why was not this call'd the *Tragedy of the Handkerchief*? What can be more absurd than (as Quintilian expresses it) *in parvis litibus has Tragoedias movere*?[5]
>
> Thomas Rymer, *A Short View of Tragedy* (1692)

From about the middle of the play, the handkerchief comes to dominate the trajectory of Othello's jealousy, and its symbolic status is underlined from the moment of its loss. Emilia tells us that it was Desdemona's 'first remembrance from the Moor' and, even as she steals it, knows that 'Poor lady, she'll run mad / When she shall lack it' (3.3.295.321–2); Othello reminds the audience that it was his 'first gift' to Desdemona (3.3.439); and Iago, in bidding Emilia steal it 'a hundred times', knows that this is the object above all others that will convince Othello to believe his lies (3.3.296). Desdemona herself, by Emilia's account, treats it as a substitute for Othello:

> she so loves the token
> – For he conjured her she should ever keep it –
> That she reserves it evermore about her
> To kiss and talk to;   (3.3.297–300)

and Othello tells contradictory stories of its origin. First it is the gift of his dying mother, a magic token, given to her by an Egyptian as a means of retaining her husband's love; later he says it is 'an antique token / My father gave my mother' (3.4.57–77; 5.2.214–15). Either way, the point is to make the audience understand its symbolic, even fetishised status. The handkerchief is not magic in Cinthio, Shakespeare's source, where it is briefly described as a gift to the lady from her husband, 'embroidered most delicately in the Moorish fashion', and does not become part of the story until Iago's plot is well advanced.[6] (This is also indicative of the different time schemes of the play and the novella. Where Cinthio's tale is extended over an unspecified period of weeks or months, *Othello*'s famous 'double time' scheme juxtaposes an apparent development over about three days with occasional references to a much longer time-scale in which Iago has time to beg Emilia a hundred times to steal the handkerchief and Cassio has time to lie with Desdemona a thousand times (3.3.296, 5.2.209–10).)[7]

Two comparisons with other plays here may help to specify the way this heavily invested prop functions in the play. First, comparison with the skull in *Hamlet* reveals not only what different kinds of props these are, but also how different the two plays are. When Hamlet holds up Yorick's skull, it is as though he and the prop step out of the play to make a more universal meaning, to invite the audience into a deliberate pause in which they contemplate the meaning of death. Actor and prop together form an iconic tableau commenting on the play and bridging the gap between the play and the concerns of the audience. The handkerchief in *Othello*, by contrast, has meaning only within the fiction, and speaks to the audience only of the play's concerns. Though it takes on a metaphysical dimension, it does not really raise any universal questions for contemplation. It does, however, recall that same popular earlier play that *Hamlet* recalls and challenges in such different ways: *The Spanish Tragedy*. Othello's handkerchief, 'Spotted with strawberries' (3.3.438; Shakespeare adds this detail to his source), recalls the 'handkercher besmeared with blood' (*Spanish Tragedy*, 2.5.50) which Hieronimo takes from his dead son's body and vows to keep with him until the act of revenge is performed. That handkerchief too becomes fetishised in the course of the play and repeatedly reappears as a reminder of wrong and an incentive to revenge.

The red spotting of the handkerchief also comes to seem ironically suggestive of blood both past and future, both the blood of lost maidenhead and the blood of Othello's murder, and Othello himself draws the parallel between sexual congress and death as he plots his revenge: 'Thy bed, lust-stained, shall with lust's blood be spotted.' (5.1.36).[8] The handkerchief symbolically becomes Desdemona's or any woman's chastity, and Shakespeare shows how Iago makes this happen:

> IAGO
> But if I give my wife a handkerchief –
>
> OTHELLO
> What then?
>
> IAGO
> Why, then, 'tis hers, my lord, and being hers
> She may, I think, bestow't on any man.
>
> OTHELLO
> She is protectress of her honour too:
> May she give that?
>
> IAGO
> Her honour is an essence that's not seen,
> They have it very oft that have it not.
> But, for the handkerchief –.   (4.1.10–18)

As Othello emphasises to Desdemona, the loss of the handkerchief spells perdition:

> Make it a darling, like your precious eye! –
> To lose't or give't away were such perdition
> As nothing else could match.   (3.4.68–70)

The terms ironically recall the fearful expression of his own love at the point where Iago's destructive work begins:

> Excellent wretch! perdition catch my soul
> But I do love thee! and when I love thee not
> Chaos is come again;   (3.3.90–2)

and chaos is exactly what does come with Othello's 'trance', as he lies on the ground raving about the handkerchief and the lying on or with Desdemona (4.1.35–43).

'The handkerchief', Rymer asserts, 'is so remote a trifle, no booby, on this side Mauritania, could make any consequence from it.'[9] At one level it is precisely the gap between the trivial nature of the object and the harm it does that constitutes both Othello's tragedy and Iago's triumph. 'O devil!' are the last words of Othello's trance, expressing a recognition, even at his most incoherent, that there is something diabolical, supernatural, about one man's will and capacity to create chaos out of nothing. Iago, like Rymer, knows that the handkerchief is a mere trifle, but knows also that its symbolic value makes it the right object for his purpose and that, in any case:

> Trifles light as air
> Are to the jealous confirmations strong
> As proofs of holy writ.   (3.3.325–7)

For Rymer, the triviality of the trigger for Othello's jealousy reduced the play's moral message to mere puerility.

> First, this may be a caution to all maidens of quality how, without their parents' consent, they run away with blackamoors.
> . . .
> Secondly, this may be a warning to all good wives, that they look well to their linen. Thirdly, this may be a lesson to husbands, that before their jealousy be tragical, the proofs may be mathematical.
>   Thomas Rymer, *A Short View of Tragedy* (1692)

But the trifling nature of the evidence is of a piece with the notorious 'motiveless malignity' of Iago.[10] If either Iago's reasons or the evidence he fakes seemed truly compelling we would be able to make more sense of the play, and it would become in turn less susceptible to the totalising discourse of good and evil that emerges out of its repeated references to angels and devils. As it is, Iago's actions bring powerful moral forces into collision within a situation so domestic as to make the horror of pure, unmotivated wickedness the more visible and the tragedy of the unwitting protagonist the more painful.

Core scene: 4.3

Act 4, scene 3, often called the willow scene, is unusual among the tragedies up to this point in being a scene almost wholly between two women. There had been scenes in *Romeo and Juliet* between Juliet and her nurse and/or her mother, but these were more plot-driven than this scene. An extended interchange between two grown women of the kind that occurs in this scene between Desdemona and Emilia is a new departure for Shakespearean tragedy, though very familiar in his comedy. (Casting of this scene affects its impact very significantly. Where two women of similar age are cast, as in Oliver Parker's film version of 1995, for example, the relationship between the women and the utterance of their very different views on what women are or can be in relation to men, makes viewers consider Emilia's views more seriously and judge Desdemona's innocence and idealism differently from versions that cast Emilia as an older woman, whose views are then seen as predicated upon greater age and experience.) It begins with a short interchange between Lodovico, Othello and Desdemona, where we see Othello's dismissal of Desdemona and her instant obedience to his command:

DESDEMONA
                    Will you walk, sir?

OTHELLO
O, Desdemona –

DESDEMONA
          My lord?

OTHELLO
                    Get you to bed
On th'instant, I will be returned forthwith.
Dismiss your attendant there: look't be done.

DESDEMONA
I will, my lord.   (4.3.4–8)

The scene follows on from a sequence that includes Othello's vicious accusations of Desdemona ('strumpet'; 'whore'; 'that cunning whore of Venice' (4.2.82, 88, 91)); Desdemona's request that Emilia should 'Lay on my bed my wedding sheets' (4.2.107); and Iago's sinister reassurance: 'Go in, and weep not; all things shall be well' (4.2.173). The audience therefore knows that Othello's command that Desdemona should dismiss Emilia is one that bodes ill.

The brief duration of this scene, then, before Desdemona dismisses Emilia, is time poignantly experienced by the audience, who understand its sweetness to have about it the pain of approaching death. This knowledge is confirmed to the audience via a calm and accepting prescience on Desdemona's part, seen first in the continued motif of the wedding sheets ('If I do die before thee, prithee shroud me / In one of these same sheets'; 4.3.22–3) and continued in the song that Desdemona sings intermittently throughout the scene. Barbary, Desdemona's mother's maid, who ran mad for love and died singing the willow song, is both reminiscent of Ophelia and ironically different from Emilia, who, as Desdemona's own maid, is much more hard-headed than Barbary. Emilia's presence also renders Desdemona less like Ophelia at this particular moment, since her sad preparation for her own death is not only not mad, but is also warmed by a female-to-female intimacy that is both physical and conversational, as Emilia unpins Desdemona for bed and the two women talk of male–female relations. In this scene, that talk scripts a contrast between realism and idealism:

> DESDEMONA
> Dost thou in conscience think – tell me, Emilia –
> That there be women do abuse their husbands
> In such gross kind?
>
> EMILIA
>   There be some such, no question.
>
> DESDEMONA
> Wouldst thou do such a deed for all the world?
>
> EMILIA
> Why, would not you?
>
> DESDEMONA
>   No, by this heavenly light!
>
> EMILIA
> Nor I neither, by this heavenly light:
> I might do't as well i' the dark.
>
> DESDEMONA
> Wouldst thou do such a deed for all the world?

EMILIA
The world's a huge thing: it is a great price
For a small vice.   (60–9)

This is the same Emilia who warned Desdemona about men in the scene where
Othello turns on Desdemona for the loss of the handkerchief:

They are all but stomachs, and we all but food:
They eat us hungerly, and when they are full
They belch us.   (3.4.105–7)

Few images could more graphically or grossly depict men as cynical users
of women, and Desdemona's faith that Othello could not be jealous looks
naïve beside it. Just as Emilia's remark closes the dialogue between herself and
Desdemona on this earlier occasion, so in the willow scene Emilia's lengthy
diatribe against husbands, her insistence that 'The ills we do, their ills instruct us
so' (102), is almost the last thing in the scene. It is followed only by Desdemona's
virtuous prayer that she herself may improve by coming into contact with
badness: 'God me such usage send / Not to pick bad from bad but by bad
mend!' (104).

Neither Desdemona nor Emilia, however, is represented consistently in the
way she is in this scene. Desdemona, naïve and idealistic about love here, has
shown an assertiveness in love that allows her to deceive her father at the start
of the play, and, more surprisingly, is capable of maintaining a knowing sexual banter with Iago about women when she first arrives in Cyprus, perhaps
thereby partly provoking Iago's offensive comment on Cassio's gallantry to her
(2.1.109–77). Emilia, more problematically, though she seems a faithful, if cynical, attendant to Desdemona in the willow scene, is in bad faith, since it is she
who has given the handkerchief to Iago at his request, in full expectation that
Desdemona will 'run mad' when she finds it gone. This untrustworthiness is
not an accidental piece of bad plotting, since Shakespeare changes the source
to produce it. Where in Cinthio Iago lifts the handkerchief from Desdemona's
girdle while she is holding his child in her arms, in Shakespeare's play Desdemona drops it and Emilia picks it up, with a speech that not only reminds the
audience how important it is to both Desdemona and Othello, but also seems
notably thin in motivation:

what he will do with it
Heaven knows, not I,
I nothing, but to please his fantasy.
(3.3.301–3)[11]

At one level, such 'inconsistency' of character is merely evidence that consistency of characterisation is not always a high priority in Renaissance drama.[12] Sometimes it is subject to another agenda, and here Shakespeare is deliberately playing up the element of chance in the plot, in order to play down the elements of rationality and human agency. (This is of a piece with the thinness of Iago's motivation and evidence, discussed above.) On the other hand, the facts that Shakespeare goes out of his way to make Emilia the mechanism whereby the handkerchief reaches Iago and that the willow scene is entirely Shakespeare's invention, may suggest that the nature of this relationship between the two women was important to his conception of the play. Its doubleness sends a chill through the seeming warmth of this scene, leaving Desdemona looking perhaps finally even more alone than the ultimately mad and solitary Ophelia.

Rhetoric and sacrifice

As double-edged and contradictory as the relationship between Desdemona and Emilia is the language that Othello speaks. We hear of him before we see him, and his language is the first thing that Iago singles out for opprobrium, in describing Othello's response to Iago's suit to become his lieutenant:

> But he, as loving his own pride and purposes,
> Evades them, with a bombast circumstance
> Horribly stuffed with epithets of war.
>
> (1.1.12–14)

Thus 'bombast', or inflated diction (literally 'stuffing'), is introduced to the audience as the essence of Othello's speech. When Othello first appears, Iago warns him that Brabantio, with whose daughter Othello has eloped, is greatly beloved and possessed of 'a voice potential / as double as the duke's'; and Othello expresses confidence about his own capacity to 'out-tongue' Brabantio (1.2.13–14, 19). When Brabantio appears with soldiers to arrest Othello, the audible lyricism of Othello's speech is both powerful and out of place: 'Keep up your bright swords, for the dew will rust them' (1.2.59). Called upon to defend himself before the senate, he protests his verbal ineptitude:

> Rude am I in my speech
> And little blest with the soft phrase of peace
>
> (1.3.82–3)

and his determination to deliver 'a round unvarnished tale' of what has taken place (the word 'tale' somewhat belying 'round' and 'unvarnished'), only for that protest to be almost immediately outfaced by his rhythmic, lyrical and persuasive narrative of his wooing of Desdemona. It is no surprise to learn that his speech is what has inspired her love. He told exotic tales of his adventures and she 'with a greedy ear' returned again and again to 'Devour up my discourse' (1.3.150–1).

Iago understands this very well, though he formulates it, characteristically, in language that besmirches the truth it purveys: 'Mark me with what violence she first loved the Moor, but for bragging and telling her fantastical lies – and will she love him still for prating?' (2.1.220–2). And yet, as 'the Othello music' develops with the play, it is noticeable that it is sometimes at odds with or in excess of the situation, like the lyrical command to put up swords, and this is sometimes made visible through dialogue with the plainer and rougher speech of Iago.[13]

> IAGO
> Patience, I say; your mind perhaps may change.
>
> OTHELLO
> Never, Iago. Like to the Pontic sea
> Whose icy current and compulsive course
> Ne'er keeps retiring ebb, but keeps due on
> To the Propontic and the Hellespont:
> Even so my bloody thoughts with violent pace
> Shall ne'er look back, ne'er ebb to humble love
> Till that a capable and wide revenge
> Swallow them up.   (3.3.455–63)

T. S. Eliot famously saw Othello as self-dramatising; and it is certainly true that the tendency to shape the tragic experience as a story, already noted in Brutus and Hamlet, is much more emphatically marked in Othello (who totally lacks Hamlet's wry self-awareness and could never joke as he does).[14] Because, too, we are made to understand throughout that Othello is wrong about the facts, his careful rhetorical fashioning of events seems the more obviously fashioned. In the same way, when Shakespeare scripts a collapse of rhetoric, as in the chaos of Othello's 'trance' (stage direction, 4.1.43), that collapse casts a shadow over the smoothness of the rhetoric around it.

Ironically, despite its beauty, Othello's speech moves towards doing the same kind of work as Iago's, for different reasons: making black white. Determined to murder Desdemona in her bed (at Iago's suggestion), Othello must use language to construct this as the right and only course of action. Like Titus Andronicus, he conceives of his own violent act as a ritual sacrifice. When he first resolves on it, his strongly aestheticised response ('Like to the Pontic sea', quoted above) is followed by a ritual vow, made kneeling; and the formally paced solemnity of this discourse and action tries to straitjacket an action which is itself chaotic into the appearance of rightness. As he enters for the final scene he immediately adopts the highly repetitive rhetoric which is to pace and formalise his violent action:

> It is the cause, it is the cause, my soul!
> . . .
> Put out the light, and then put out the light!
>   (5.2.1,7)

but Desdemona's continued affirmation of her innocence disrupts the smooth flow of a supposedly just revenge, arousing Othello's anger:

> O perjured woman, thou dost stone my heart
> And makest me call what I intend to do
> A murder, which I thought a sacrifice!
>   (5.2.63–5)

The mode of the killing, smothering Desdemona in her bed (a further alteration to the source), though welcomed by Othello for its capacity to construct the murder as a proper ritual, is also an act which physically represents Othello's oppression of innocence, as the sheer weight of his body crushes Desdemona's and hides it from view. Its effect is very different from the climactic thrust of an avenging sword into the right body. Even *Hamlet*, for all its concentration on accident in the last scene, gives the audience the brief satisfaction of seeing Hamlet give Claudius a fatal wound with the poisoned foil.

Not surprisingly, *Othello* goes further than *Hamlet* in its dramatisation of botches and failures. Othello's conspiracy with Iago to kill Cassio, whom he thinks is the man who has wronged him, merely wounds him in the leg. His attempts to kill Iago, when he finally realises him to be the man who has really wronged him, are even more humiliating. He first runs at him, only to be disarmed by Montano, while Iago escapes; and when Iago is brought back a prisoner, he tries again to stab him but fails, anticipating his own failure with the line that makes excuse for it: 'If that thou be'st a devil, I cannot kill thee' (5.2.284). Most outrageously of all, he kills himself, recognising himself thereby as the only proper object of his own revenge. The whole emptiness and futility of his imagined revenge on his innocent wife is contained in the circularity of this final act of violence, a ritualised mimicry of his botched revenge:

> I kissed thee ere I killed thee: no way but this,
> Killing myself, to die upon a kiss.
>
> (5.2.356–7)

Such false imposition of pattern on accident and ineptitude also measures this play's distance from *Romeo and Juliet*. While both plays construct a sense that the tragic outcome could easily have been avoided, in the earlier play the lovers are beset by a combination of chance and outside forces over which they have no control, whereas in *Othello* the forces that lead towards tragedy are entirely human, despite Othello's attempt to outlaw Iago as non-human.

Yet the creation of pattern is also necessary to give the tragedy shape. The mimicry of Desdemona's murder by Othello's suicide brings a sense of closure at least, if not atonement, to the outrage of that wrongful and unnecessary death and emphasises the intensity of the bond between the lovers. The very unnecessariness of Desdemona's death becomes the ground for the necessity of Othello's.

Chapter 7

Timon of Athens

Timon of Athens is a play rarely performed and rarely treated with the same seriousness as Shakespeare's other tragedies, for a number of reasons. First, it is widely accepted as having been co-written with Thomas Middleton, and may also be unfinished.[1] (These possibilities are not mutually exclusive, as some scholars seem to suggest.) Its status is further called into question by the fact that it seems to be slotted into the place in the First Folio originally intended for *Troilus and Cressida*. Together with *Antony and Cleopatra*, it is also one of two plays in the First Folio not divided into acts or scenes.[2] Its date too is substantially in doubt, with suggestions ranging anywhere from 1603 to 1609. There is no evidence of any early performance of the play, and dating is based entirely on stylistic evidence, which in turn partly depends on the question of authorship.[3] Given its similarities with *King Lear* and the parallels between Middleton's conjectured share of the play and Middleton's other works, a date between 1604 and 1606 seems most likely (though there is no agreement as to which of *Timon* or *Lear* came first). Shakespeare here returns to Plutarch, though the play is not based, as the Roman plays are, on any one or more of Plutarch's full-length 'Lives', but worked up from short passages in the Lives of Antony and Alcibiades together with Lucian's *Dialogue of Timon*.[4]

Allegory and pageant

Despite its many parallels with *King Lear*, however, *The Life of Timon of Athens* is more striking for its difference than for its resemblances to other Shakespearean tragedies. In particular it seems to owe much more to the medieval and early Tudor tradition of allegorical drama than do any of Shakespeare's other tragedies. Indeed its title marks it out as different (other Shakespearean tragedies are normally called 'The Tragedy of' or 'The Life and Death of' the protagonists concerned) and suggests a closer alignment with earlier drama focusing on the moral life of an everyman-figure.[5] That debt is evident from the opening scene, which brings together a Poet, a Painter, a Jeweller and a

Merchant, all 'glib and slipp'ry creatures' (1.54) visibly emblematic of greed and hypocrisy, as they discuss what they have brought for Timon, their rich patron.[6] In Jonathan Miller's 1981 BBC television production the well-known television satirists John Fortune and John Bird played the Poet and the Painter.

The bringing together of representative figures to enact an emblematic scenario is strongly reminiscent of earlier drama, and this emblematic quality becomes particularly striking in the extended development of the image of Fortune's hill, which focuses the whole shape of what is to come in the play in a clearly didactic manner, rather resembling a chorus. The realistic excuse for the speech is the Poet's account of his poem; but his description of Fortune enthroned on a hill, surrounded by 'all deserts, all kind of natures' (1.66), is a very familiar image from both medieval and classical literary tradition, and is represented on stage in the early Elizabethan interlude *Liberality and Prodigality* (*c.* 1567–8). It also featured in the coronation pageants for King James in 1604, crowning the triumphal arch which represented the Garden of Plenty.[7] As the Poet develops the image, Fortune favours one 'of Lord Timon's frame' (70), who climbs to the top of the hill and is immediately surrounded by fawning followers, seeking access to 'the free air' (84) of the hill-top through him; but Fortune characteristically changes her mood to spurn Timon, and his followers are content to let him fall unaided. As the painter rightly responds to this narrative, ''Tis common' (90); in other words, both the experience of 'The foot above the head' (95) and the choice of it as a subject for art are truisms.

Allegorical morality drama, popular from the fifteenth century, specialised in dramatising obvious forms of human failing or fall, aiming not to surprise by originality but to underline and reinforce the teachings of the church. The point was not to create a new image but to recreate a familiar image in an especially forceful way. Such dramatic forms retained their hold over popular audiences well into Shakespeare's lifetime, and Marlowe's *Dr Faustus*, for example, shows how it was also possible to wrench these older forms into new meanings in the context of the new scepticism and secularism stimulated by the Reformation and the demise of a long-held collective system of belief. Indeed the Poet's image of Fortune, a microcosmic preview of the structure of the play, strongly resembles the opening chorus of *Faustus*, which outlines Faustus' fall before the play proper begins. The thinking underlying both is that spectators will pay closer attention to the detail of how error leads to fall if they know in advance that this is the shape of what they are looking at. As critics have noted, the plot of *Timon of Athens* is unusually schematic, echoing the rise and fall pattern of morality drama, with narrative elements and lines spoken in the second half paralleling elements in the first.[8]

Timon himself lacks individuality by comparison with Shakespeare's other tragic heroes, and in this way resembles an Everyman- or Mankind-figure, a quasi-empty vehicle. The play does not flesh him out with a family or a history. Unlike *Othello*, where the sense of a rich and crucially shaping past is regularly invoked, this play seems to create a present moment which comes out of nowhere. It is also curiously static in the second half: characters come to visit Timon in the woods like figures in a pageant, creating a sequence of tableaux, and seem to relate only to him rather than to each other.[9] Stage-pictures and verbal utterance sometimes highlight its emblematic quality. Wielding his spade, for example, once he has turned his back on the city and withdrawn into the woods, Timon resembles the central figure of the morality play *Mankind* (1465–70), beating away temptation; a figure in turn based upon the biblical figure of Adam, digging the earth in the sweat of his brow (Genesis, 3.17–19).[10] Hounded by his creditors, Timon resembles the figure of Hospitality pursued by Usury in Robert Wilson's *Three Ladies of London* (c. 1581). Inviting Athenians to come and hang themselves on a tree in the wood, his words recall the traditional figure of Despair, with rope and dagger (14.740–7).[11] Making a strong 'I am' statement, he seems less the self-affirming tragic hero asserting his presence than the actor of medieval allegory announcing his role: 'I am *Misanthropos*, and hate mankind' (14.53).

Yet this very sequence of positions (mankind; hospitality; despair; misanthrope) demonstrates a fluidity about Timon's role which is very far from the fixity that individual moments suggest, a fixity necessary for the effective functioning of allegory. Whereas the didactic function of an interlude like *Liberality and Prodigality*, for example, relies on a clear distinction throughout between the two title-roles, *Timon* constructs a central protagonist who seems to hover between both of these alternatives in an ambiguous moral state. The greed and hypocrisy of Timon's followers is self-evident, but Timon's own fault, referred to early on as 'riot' (prodigality) by his faithful steward (4.3), is also described by that same steward as an excess of liberality in a much longer soliloquy that ponders the injustice of Timon's fate: 'Strange, unusual blood / When man's worst sin is he does too much good!' (13.38–9). The Timon of contemporary popular tradition was a stock misanthrope. As John Draper argued in 1934, Shakespeare's particular take on his sources was to inflect them towards the 'fundamental paradox' of 'a bankrupt wastrel whose downfall we are expected to lament'.[12]

Even as seemingly allegorical tableaux are set up, they are undercut by the script. The stage picture of Timon digging, for example, looks like an allegorical figure of virtuous labour, but the venomous diatribe against the earth that he utters as he digs complicates the image, positioning him almost outside mankind rather than of it: 'His semblable, yea, himself, Timon disdains. / Destruction fang mankind' (14.22–3). The gold, too, functions in a more complex way than it typically does in medieval plays and stories, where it almost always symbolises avarice or the transience of worldly wealth. Goods in *Everyman* (*c.* 1510–19?), locked in chests and 'sacked in bags', tells Everyman he cannot accompany him to the grave; Money in *All For Money* (*c.* 1572–7), dressed in a gown '*having the coin of silver and gold painted upon it*', boasts that 'Each lord and knight for me will fight / And hazard to be slain'.[13] Timon, however, again complicates the traditional iconography by inveighing against the gold in front of him rather than adoring it. Potentially adoring utterance is tested out only to be discarded: 'Yellow, glittering, precious gold? / No, gods, I am no idle votarist' (14.26–7).[14] Instead, Timon knows gold to be the 'yellow slave' that 'knit[s] and break[s] religions' (14.34–5). Timon thus functions as both protagonist and commentator: though he digs like Mankind, he addresses gold as though he were the preacher warning Mankind. The famous performance of the well-known critic Wilson Knight in the role of Timon sought to retain something of this emblematic quality, but revealed the difficulty of getting the tone right in a later age. His stage direction for Timon's last words to the Athenian senators before he dies runs as follows: '*Timon loosens his loin-cloth and holds it dangling in his left hand. Lights lower slightly or are concentrated with shadows. Timon wears a gold sex-covering.*'[15]

The play also has its separate commentator beyond Timon, however. Apemantus (whose name means 'feeling no pain') is a very sour and secular version of the medieval preacher, warning Timon against the error of his ways and spitting venom against mankind before Timon himself does.[16] The stage direction introducing him scripts his apartness very clearly: '*Then comes, dropping after all, Apemantus, discontentedly, like himself*' (2, opening stage direction); and he is a direct descendant of earlier malcontents and villains, melancholic, snarling on the sidelines and refusing to become a participant in any communal activity. His characteristic mode of speech is the aside: 'what a number of men eats Timon, and he sees 'em not! It grieves me to see so many dip their meat in one man's blood; and all the madness is, he cheers them up, too' (2.39–42). Like Jaques in *As You Like It*, the only figure whose company he actively welcomes is the Fool (4.51–117). Like Hamlet, he comments cynically on the action of the plot. (The repeated reference to him as a dog is partly a way of drawing attention to his position as a cynic, since the Greek term 'cynic' was widely known to mean 'dog-like'.)[17] His presence contributes to creating a critical distance between the audience and the represented action of the play, as opposed to allowing them to become immersed in an empathetic response.

Other figures besides Timon and Apemantus also function partly as types. Some of these, such as the faithful servant, Timon's steward, have a biblical resonance (and indeed the second half of the play sometimes takes on an apoc-alyptic tone); while those who assemble in the first scene have more affinity with the kind of satire in which Shakespeare's contemporary, Ben Jonson, excelled, where characters like Volpone (the fox) and Mosca (the fly, or parasite) behave according to their names. Such satirising of human types was also characteristic of city comedy, a genre that flourished in the first decade of the seventeenth cen-tury and in which Middleton particularly excelled. (Shakespeare did not write city comedy and never located his plays in contemporary London, though a location like *Julius Caesar*'s Rome or *Measure for Measure*'s Vienna can func-tion as an intermittent metaphor for it.) Female roles in the play are almost wholly typecast as whores. The only other female parts are the ladies dressed as Amazons in the masque staged at the first banquet. It is as though the bitter side of Hamlet's invective against women were allowed to stand as the only representation of female nature.[18]

Core scene: 3.6

The scene selected for analysis here is once again a banquet. As in *Titus Andron-icus*, a banquet is used twice in the play, and on the second occasion it figures as a setting for revenge, though the revenge in *Timon* is symbolic rather than bloody. In order to understand the banquet of 3.6 it is necessary to look first at how feasting has already figured in the play. It is introduced in the opening scene, when Timon invites Apemantus to dinner and he refuses:

> TIMON
> Wilt dine with me, Apemantus?
>
> APEMANTUS
> No, I eat not lords.   (1.207–8)

His answer, suggesting that Timon's guests consume him more than they do the food, puts in place a critical perspective that informs the way the audience views the scene of the first banquet (probably written by Middleton), which follows at scene 2. This is a scene which has similarities with the opening scene of *King Lear* in its juxtaposition of Timon's naïveté with the false and flattering rhetoric of his guests, but *Timon* constructs a much more black-and-white opposition between Timon and his flatterers than does *Lear*, a contrast in keeping with its allegorical style. Thus the more Timon's guests embellish their praise of Timon's generosity, the more Timon's own speeches formulate an extreme, almost unbelievable benevolence:

You mistake my love.
I gave it freely ever, and there's none
Can truly say he gives if he receives.

(2.9–11)

'O you gods,' think I, 'what need we have any friends if we should ne'er have need of 'em? They were the most needless creatures living, should we ne'er have use for 'em, and would most resemble sweet instruments hung up in cases, that keeps their sounds to themselves.' Why, I have often wished myself poorer, that I might come nearer to you. We are born to do benefits; and what better or properer can we call our own than the riches of our friends?   (2.91–9)

Set against this excessive faith in the goodness of mankind is Apemantus' excess of bile, expressly reminiscent of the image of 'The foot above the head' in the opening parable of Fortune's hill:

Who lives that's not depraved or depraves?
Who dies that bears not one spurn to their graves
Of their friends' gift?
I should fear those that dance before me now
Would one day stamp upon me.   (2.136–40)

Apemantus' occupation of a separate table on a separate part of the stage puts the image of the banquet into stage quotation marks, allowing it to be 'viewed at one remove, as a precious, self-indulgent, but entirely untrustworthy occasion'.[19] The traditional qualities represented by a banquet, hospitality and festive unity, are disrupted by the presence of a table apart occupied by a hostile commentator. In between Timon's philanthropy and Apemantus' misanthropy is the more moving and more quietly stated vision of Timon's Steward, who tries to tell Timon his fortune no longer exists and 'bleed[s] inwardly' for him (2.205). It is Apemantus' fear that Timon will 'give away thyself in paper shortly' (2.244) which closes the scene, however, and is virtually true even as Apemantus speaks.

By the time the second banquet takes place, Timon has confronted the full extent of his losses, has sent to his friends for help and been refused everywhere, and faces destitution. The scene of this second banquet shows Shakespeare and Middleton working together: while mainly written by Shakespeare, it also includes contributions from Middleton, notably the closing comic section where the guests try to retrieve their possessions. It opens with the false friends wondering whether the feast indicates that Timon's situation is not so bad after all and discussing the insistence of Timon's invitations to this feast.

Their insincerity is underlined by the juxtaposition of their easy expressions of regret at not being able to lend him the money he asked for with their comparison of the amounts required. When Timon comes in, the distance he has travelled from the earlier banqueting scene is evident in the way he now responds to flattery with a knowing aside:

> SECOND SENATOR
> The swallow follows not summer more willingly than we your lordship.
>
> TIMON [*aside*]
> Nor more willingly leaves winter, such summer birds are men.
>
> (11.28–31)

The banquet is brought in in covered dishes, prompting the greedy guests to deduce an especially lavish occasion:

> SECOND SENATOR
> All covered dishes.
>
> FIRST SENATOR
> Royal cheer, I warrant you.
>
> (47–8)

and to express the confidence that 'This is the old man still' (60).

Timon's urging of his guests not to make 'a City feast of it, to let the meat cool ere we can agree upon the first place' (66–7) seems to urge friendship over ceremony; but the grace he utters moves towards an increasingly clear expression of what Timon has learned about men, culminating in the outright equation of his so-called friends with nothingness: 'For these my present friends, as they are to me nothing, so in nothing bless them; and to nothing are they welcome' (81–3). The absence of ceremony, which seemed an index of friendship, becomes a calculated and hostile disruption of ceremony as the dishes are uncovered; and as water is revealed in place of food, Timon's carefully controlled and escalating hostility turns into uncontrolled abuse. He hurls the water in his guests' faces and allows his language to degenerate into a catalogue of insults:

> Most smiling, smooth, detested parasites,
> Courteous destroyers, affable wolves, meek bears,
> You fools of fortune, trencher-friends, time's flies,
> Cap-and-knee slaves, vapours, and minute-jacks!
>
> (93–6)

The whole rhythm of the scene changes, and what seemed to be a slowly building ceremonial scene is brought to an abrupt end as Timon exits with a violent and total rejection of his home, his city and all mankind:

> Burn house! Sink Athens! Henceforth hated be
> Of Timon man and all humanity!   (103–4)

His rage is given a more intense impact by the fact that it tears through a scene that should have been stately, ordered and festive.

The closing rhyme of Timon's diatribe seems to signal the end of the scene, but Middleton adds a telling satiric coda in which the lords scrabble for their caps and gowns and even a jewel Timon has given one of them, scattered around the stage as they themselves have scattered before Timon's fury.[20] Even at this climactic turning point for Timon, where he leaves everything and everyone he has known, his false friends are still scrabbling for their material goods. As they pronounce Timon mad, it is less with sympathy than with smug dismissal, and the scene's closing rhyme focuses not on Timon's rejection of humanity but on the continuing materialistic inhumanity of those he leaves behind:

> SECOND SENATOR
> Lord Timon's mad.
>
> THIRD SENATOR
>   I feel't upon my bones.
>
> FOURTH SENATOR
> One day he gives us diamonds, next day stones.
>   (113–14)[21]

City and forest

When we next see Timon he is outside the city wall and alone, cursing everything within it. The tiring-house wall at the back of the Elizabethan stage often represented a city wall, and was regularly used in battle scenes to create a strong sense of two groups, united against one another within their separate groupings, one of whom the audience was invited to identify with (the English in Shakespeare's history plays, for example). The placing of a solitary individual outside the city wall, however, had a very different and powerful effect, partly deriving from its contrast with those regular scenes showing the communality of a society at war. The individual outside society, also a focus of *Coriolanus*, is here a contradictory figure: on the one hand representing a moral stance against human error; but on the other representing a rejection of humanity so absolute as to mark him out as inhuman.[22] The question of location thus becomes crucially symbolic of the subjectivity depicted. A comparison with those comedies which locate part of the action in a forest or 'green world' helps to point up the way in which the use of location functions differently here. In plays such as *A Midsummer Night's Dream* and *As You Like It*, characters who face problems and conflicts at home in court or city set off for the forest and find it to be a space in which conflicts can be resolved, often in surreal or dreamlike ways. Indeed the forest feast in *As You Like It* becomes a way of figuring the opposition between the harsh and unforgiving values of the court society and the bounteous liberality of human beings living in the utopian green world (akin to the classical 'golden world' of idealised communal living).

These comedies, with their focus on alternative sets of values, signal a concern with changing values that becomes more acute as city comedy develops and as Shakespeare's own writing moves further away from romantic comedies, through *Measure for Measure c.* 1603 (the closest Shakespeare came to writing city comedy) to *Timon of Athens*. This developing sense of a crisis in values was linked both to the change of reigns and to economic changes beyond the control of any individual. Where Elizabeth I had been notable for her parsimony, James I, who came to the throne in 1603, was a prodigal spender, known for excessive gifts to his favourites and later to be in prolonged dispute with Parliament in his attempt to secure a greater income for himself and his family. Prior to James' accession, a financial crisis was already developing for the country's aristocracy, many of whom financed their life-styles, including their gift-giving, through credit; and proclamations from both reigns show increasing concern about the decay of hospitality, the duty whereby the lords of great households took a charitable interest in their local communities. Wilson's *Three Ladies of London*, mentioned above as offering a precedent for moralising Timon as Hospitality pursued by Usury, inveighs against the way the hounding of Hospitality to his death impacts upon the poor, the orphaned and the disabled.[23]

One way of reading the uncertain moral emphasis of *Timon of Athens* is in terms of the tension between old and new cultural values. While an older ethos revered the duty of hospitality as central to the maintenance of social harmony, a newer mindset recognised such values as the last remnants of an essentially feudal social structure. This can be read in terms of the mutually oppositional meanings of the word 'bond' in the play, which signifies both the natural ties of friendship and humanity that bind men together (as when Timon says his gift to a servant fulfils 'a bond in men' (1.148)) and the paper bonds recording debts that Timon's false friends call in without respect for those deeper bonds (as in scene 3). The shift from one value-system to the other is especially strongly focused in the moment of Timon's rage at finding his doors, which have always been open to all comers in a standing gesture of hospitality, now locked to keep creditors out (8.77–82). 'Housekeeping', the traditional term for such hospitality, has changed from a keeping open to a keeping closed. A changing society in which individuals could make their way out of the social class into which they were born through ability, capitalist enterprise or sharp practice recognised that country-house hospitality had no place within the social structure of expanding urban areas. The flight to the forest of Shakespeare's romantic comedies represents a partly nostalgic look at this older ethos (though in fact the forest is not a wholly benign environment in these plays, being sometimes fraught with deception and assailed by wind and rain as well as enabling certain kinds of freedom). Timon, however, flees the city not to a utopian community but first to the solitude of the woods and thence to a cave by the seashore. In place of the feasts he has learned to distrust as gatherings of hypocrites, he seeks the satisfaction of roots dug up and consumed alone; and, in an echo of Apemantus' early observation that Timon's guests eat him, Timon imagines eating such roots as eating Athens: 'That the whole life of Athens were in this! / Thus would I eat it' (14.284–5). When Apemantus, who is with him, offers Timon food to 'mend' his 'feast', Timon's response is absolute and implacable: 'First mend my company: take away thyself' (285–6).

A tragic hero?

The satiric shape of this trajectory, and indeed the driving fantasy of revenge on Athens, as against the benign comic trajectory embodied in the green-world plays, is evident. Even city comedy, so far from Shakespeare's romantic comedies in tone and so much closer to *Timon* in both tone and content, usually reaches some kind of resolution or reconciliation, however compromised. The bitterness of *Timon* and its drive towards death differentiate it finally from comic, satiric or moral drama. The cave, a place representative of complete withdrawal, shows Timon's rejection of Athens as the beginning of the path to his own death. However corrupt civic society may be, outside it there is no place for a human being to be fully human. Comfort lies in nothingness:

> My long sickness
> Of health and living now begins to mend,
> And nothing brings me all things;
>
> (14.721–3)

but nothingness is the end of living. Timon, the only one of Shakespeare's tragic heroes to write his own epitaph in advance of his death and to die offstage, truly becomes nothing in death, and no longer recognises any distinction between man and beast:

> 'Timon is dead, who hath outstretched his span.
> Some beast read this; there does not live a man.'
>
> $(16.3-4)^{24}$

Alcibiades' role in the play is partly to show another way of reacting to a seemingly ungrateful city and a newer set of values. Instead of withdrawing to solipsistic isolation as Timon does, he leaves the city in order to gather together an army with which to take it by force. Although his use of force is partly a personal revenge, he is nevertheless represented as a force for order, since he guarantees to punish only those who have merited punishment, to maintain justice under the law and to 'Make war breed peace, make peace stint war' (17.56–63, 84). Like Fortinbras in *Hamlet*, he brings the play to closure by acknowledging Timon's nobility and issuing a command to his soldiers: 'Let our drums strike' (17.86).

But how does Timon's claim to nobility compare with that of a figure such as Hamlet? Does he fulfil the role of tragic hero? His curious neutrality, or absence of individuality, emerging out of the play's emblematic and satiric dramaturgy, is one problem in the way of acknowledging either Timon or the play as tragic or heroic. A recurrent benchmark for the tragic hero in the tragedies discussed up to this point has been the question of what it is to be a man. Romeo is rebuked by the Friar for not being a man; the peak of Antony's praise for Brutus is that 'This was a man!'; and Hamlet remembers his own father above all in these terms: 'A was a man, take him for all in all: / I shall not look upon his like again' (1.2.187–8). Manhood in the tragedies is sometimes a matter of virility and sometimes a broader issue of humanity itself. Othello comes close to losing both when he lies raving uncontrollably on the ground; but Timon's conscious and absolute rejection of humanity represents new ground in Shakespearean tragedy. The words 'man' and 'mankind' are relentlessly repeated in the play, so that the intensity of this play's concern with the subject is foregrounded. Alcibiades, asking Timon's name, is shocked that man can be 'so hateful to thee / That art thyself a man?' (14.51–2); Timon in turn wishes Alcibiades were a dog, so that he might love him a little (14.54–5); but the faithful Steward, who shares all he has with Timon's other servants when the household breaks up and vows to serve Timon with his life, is the figure who truly calls Timon's rejection of all mankind into question. 'How fain would I have hated all mankind,' Timon laments, 'And thou redeem'st thyself!' (14.498–9). In offering Timon faithful, unconditional service, the Steward becomes a type of humanity not driven by money and not elsewhere represented in Timon's Athens. In refusing to accept the comfort the Steward offers or to allow the evidence of the Steward's loyalty to inflect his view of humanity, Timon puts himself beyond the pale.[25] The Steward becomes the play's clearest instance of unqualified nobility, while Timon is reduced by his failure to accommodate to that nobility. He remains suspended between emblematic and tragic status. Though Alcibiades calls Timon noble, the play does not finally demonstrate that nobility. Timon does not find the greatness of heart to recognise what it is to be a man before he dies.

Chapter 8

King Lear

King Lear survives in two versions. These are sufficiently different from one another to have persuaded several recent editors to print them independently rather than to draw on both to produce a conflated text, as has been common practice in editing Shakespeare's plays generally.[1] The title page of the 1608 Quarto printing tells us that the play was performed 'before the King's majesty at Whitehall upon St Stephen's night in Christmas holidays', and stationers' records confirm the date of this performance as 26 December 1606. Some version of the play, therefore was complete by late 1606, but how far that version may have corresponded to either of the extant printed texts remains a matter for debate. I have chosen to follow the Quarto text here, in the probability that more of its text represents the earliest version of the play, which is the version that would place it at this point in the chronology of Shakespeare's tragedy, close to *Timon*. But even this argument is open to doubt. The play may have been subject to both revision and censorship, and it is likely that no single text simultaneously comes closest to what was first written and what was first performed. What Shakespeare first wrote may have been revised by him, on aesthetic or theatrical grounds, but may equally have been revised or censored by others for printing or performance on political grounds; and the Folio, despite being printed so much later than the Quarto, may yet record elements of an earlier text than appears in the Quarto.[2]

Unclear as the textual circumstances are, what emerges from them is a political play performed in a politically sensitive environment, before King James and the court, by the company which the King had honoured with his name. A play about a king who gives up the right to rule and divides his kingdom between the Dukes of Cornwall and Albany, thereby provoking civil war, would be politically sensitive at any time; but played before a King of England who was also King of Scotland, who held and had published strong views on the divine right of kings, who had been pressing parliament to ratify a united kingdom of Great Britain since his accession in 1603 and whose sons were the Dukes of Cornwall (Henry) and Albany (Charles), its political sensitivity was even more clearly marked.[3] Given, furthermore, that conspirators in the Gunpowder Plot

had sought to assassinate King and parliament and had been executed for treason in January 1606, and that parliament was currently debating whether a
king's subjects owed allegiance to him or to the country, a play representing
civil war, differing kinds of allegiance and various kinds of insult and affront
to an anointed king had even more immediate reason to tread carefully. That
the play channeled so much criticism of its King through his fool, when James
himself was known to have an especial affection for his official fool, Archie
Armstrong, made its potential allusiveness all the more pointed.

Tragedy of state

Lear, as already noted in chapter 7 above, has many parallels with *Timon of
Athens*, including a deep concern with the bonds that bind human society
together. But where *Timon* explores these bonds predominantly through the
experience of one individual, *Lear* broadens the plot to make that concern
central to a whole range of characters and relationships. Indeed one of Shakespeare's many alterations to the source play, the anonymous *True Chronicle
History of King Leir* (*c.* 1588–94) was to add a subplot (the story of Gloucester
and his sons) for the first time in his tragedy, drawing on a story from Sidney's
Arcadia. The first scene of the play uses both plots to juxtapose a focus on
family bonds, legitimate and illegitimate, with a focus on the broader social
and political bonds underpinning the state. It opens with Kent and Gloucester
discussing the forthcoming 'division of the kingdoms' (1.1.4) and the King's
disposition towards the Dukes of Albany and Cornwall, then moves to a discussion of Gloucester's two sons, the bastard or 'natural' son Edmund and the
legitimate Edgar. When the King and court enter, this move from the political
to the personal (possibly a strategic one to avoid too direct a political charge
in the play) is re-enacted as Lear first calls for the map to exhibit the planned
division of the kingdom, then moves to a much more personal (and absurdly
inappropriate) focus: a love-test, designed to confirm the proposed division.
Cordelia's answer to the question 'Which of you shall we say doth love us most?'
(1.1.44) affirms that she loves her father 'According to my bond, nor more nor
less' (1.1.83), but the plainness of this, by contrast with the 'glib and oily art'
(1.1.213) of her sisters, renders her response unacceptable to Lear. Despite
Kent's attempt to honour the bond of service he owes to his master by warning
him against rash action, Lear ruptures the bond between father and daughter
by banishing Cordelia, thus setting in motion the play's extended examination
of how bonds are maintained or broken between human beings.

But even before Lear ruptures the bond between father and daughter, he has
already ruptured the bond between the monarch and his people by dividing

his kingdom. Speeches by both James and Elizabeth used family metaphors to figure the monarch's relation to the kingdom. In a speech delivered to his first parliament in March 1604 on the need for union between England and Scotland, James said: 'What God hath conjoined then, let no man separate. I am the husband, and all the whole isle is my lawful wife'.[4] Some productions have emphasised the violence and destructiveness of the rupture by having Lear physically tear up the map. Shakespeare is again shaping his source quite radically here, since the old *King Leir* does not include any such decision to divide the kingdom. But in Shakespeare's play, with its moments of apocalyptic vision, one bond is linked to another, and each individual rupture takes its place within a more widespread and terrifying disruption: 'Love cools, friendship falls off, brothers divide: in cities mutinies, in countries discords, palaces treason, the bond cracked between son and father' (1.2.100–2). Again the function of the subplot is to widen, even universalise, the particular individual experience (the prophecy recalls the Bible, Matthew 24). But, where individual offences may be forgiven and remedied, the offence against the kingdom cannot.[5] And such offence also ruptures the self, as Lear soon begins to recognise: 'Who is it that can tell me who I am? / Lear's shadow' (1.4.218–19).[6] The distance between this and the heroic, sometimes posturing 'I am' of earlier tragic heroes, demonstrates a changing conception of the tragic hero ongoing from *Othello* and *Timon of Athens*. Such uncompromising boldness becomes increasingly the province of the villain: 'Edmund the base shall to th'legitimate./ I grow, I prosper. Now gods, stand up for bastards!' (1.2.20–1).

Lear, by contrast, must learn humility, and must learn that his offence against the kingdom is not just political, in the sense that he makes a wrong decision about how to govern, but also ethical and humanitarian, in that he comes to understand his own responsibility for rooted social injustice. Shut out of doors in the storm, he has to confront the defencelessness of 'Poor naked wretches' and to realise that he has 'ta'en / Too little care of this' (3.4.24, 28–9). The subplot echoes this same discovery as Gloucester hands over a purse to Poor Tom, telling him that 'distribution should undo excess, / And each man have enough' (4.1.68–9). Pomp such as kings and courtiers cultivate is culpable because it perpetuates social injustice and real need:

> Take physic, pomp,
> Expose thyself to feel what wretches feel,
> That thou mayst shake the superflux to them
> And show the heavens more just;
>
> (3.4.29–32)

and need is something Lear has already been driven to consider very minutely by his daughters' stripping of his retinue. As each daughter gradually reduces the number of knights she will allow until Regan reaches the nadir of 'What needs one?', Lear is driven to his great outburst against such pinching meanness: 'O, reason not the need: our basest beggars / Are in the poorest thing superfluous' (2.4.233–5). The turn away from an attack on courtly extravagance, which would have been highly pointed if performed at Whitehall, may again have had a strategic as well as a moral point.

The play thus forces together two harshly linked confrontations, with emotional and with physical need. Lear first learns what it is to be rejected and treated with cruelty by thankless children and then, as a consequence of that cruelty, what it is to be reduced to a 'poor, bare, forked animal' (3.4.96) in need of warmth and shelter. The second recognition, of the importance of responding to a man's most basic physical needs, stands in tense relation to the first, that being human cannot be reduced to the mere sum of these needs; but it does not cancel it out. Though human beings must demonstrate their shared humanity by taking care of one another at the most basic level, they must also recognise that love and respect produce further obligations, and that trampling such obligations is a form of inhumanity. Lear calls his daughters monsters before they shut their doors on him. It is their attempt to strip him of his self-respect that bemonsters them.

Comparison with *Timon* is also instructive in interpreting the progress of Lear's understanding. Timon starts out with a more naïve and idealistic view of human nature than Lear, believing that 'we are born to do benefits' and that friends exist to fulfil one another's needs (2.91–9); he keeps hospitality in the traditional sense, by keeping his doors always open, and is outraged to find his doors locking him in and others out; he discovers that men are flatterers by nature ('men are the things themselves', he answers in response to Apemantus' question 'What things in the world canst thou nearest compare to thy flatterers?' (14.318–21)); and he finally rejects all humanity, including his faithful steward, choosing nakedness and nothingness over life. Lear, by contrast, has to learn that human beings have a duty to fulfil one another's needs; he finds himself locked out of doors rather than in, and comes as a consequence not only to discover what his most basic needs are, but also that there are those who will sacrifice their own needs to fulfil them for him and those who would willingly let him die. In reaching the realisation that 'the thing itself' is '[u]naccommodated man' (3.4.95) and that, even at that lowest ebb, such wretches can help and comfort one another, he goes mad; but he also survives and partly recovers.

If *King Lear* is pessimistic, its pessimism is of a very different kind from *Timon*'s, where the hero straightforwardly rejects humanity and welcomes death. *Lear* forces its hero to take on a transformed set of values. Where Timon retreats to his cave as an escape from humanity (having never known 'the middle of humanity', as Apemantus comments, but only 'the extremity of both ends' (14.302–3)), Lear shares the shelter of a hovel with Kent, the Fool and Poor Tom (Edgar), and reaches an understanding of what this means:

> Where is this straw, my fellow?
> The art of our necessities is strange,
> That can make vile things precious. Come, your hovel.
>
> (3.2.69–71)

The structure of the play does not permit him, as the structure of *Timon* does permit its central protagonist, to ignore the possibility of human kindness. The presence of Timon's steward is multiplied in *Lear* not only by the presence of Cordelia, Kent, Edgar and the Fool, but also by three nameless faithful servants who change the course of events in the subplot.

Core scene: 3.7

The yoking together of humanity with hideous inhumanity, and the duty to see both clearly, are nowhere more succinctly and emblematically represented than in the blinding of Gloucester. The scene opens showing Cornwall's hard efficiency, and moves with astonishing speed to the intensified viciousness of Regan and Goneril:

> CORNWALL [*to Goneril*]
> Post speedily to my lord your husband; show him this letter. The army of France is landed. Seek out the villain Gloucester.
>
> [*Exeunt some Servants*]
>
> REGAN
> Hang him instantly.
>
> GONERIL
> Pluck out his eyes.   (3.7.1–4)

It is this automatic instinct towards violence that Edward Bond takes as the basis of his rewriting of the play, the recognition expressed a little later in Shakespeare's play by Albany that 'Humanity must perforce prey on itself / Like monsters of the deep' (4.2.47–8). When Goneril turns Albany's perception into an attack on his manhood ('Marry your manhood. Mew' (4.2.66)), we may be reminded of the continuing concern with what manhood is throughout Shakespearean tragedy, and the specific concern here to distinguish between honourable virility and monstrous aggression.[7] Deeds of violence performed for their own sake, this play emphasises, take a man beyond the pale of humanity; and ironically this point is rendered most clearly through the inhumanity of two female figures.

Cornwall's concern that Edmund should leave, since '[t]he revenges we are bound to take upon your traitorous father are not fit for your beholding' (7–8), reminds the audience of a son who, unknown to Cornwall, is as vicious as these daughters, again broadening the single family's unnaturalness into a wider truth about human relations. Both families in the play mix children loyal to their bonds with those who delight in breaking them. Oswald's brief presence in this scene also functions by way of parallel: as a type of the false servant, 'the composition of a knave, beggar, coward, pander, and the son and heir of a mongrel bitch' (2.2.18–20), he anticipates in reverse the model of faithful service which is to become the core of this scene. His earlier insulting and disrespectful behaviour towards Lear, furthermore, is recalled in the deliberate degradation of Gloucester which follows here, as Cornwall orders him to be pinioned like a thief and Regan plucks him by the beard. Indeed Gloucester's initial reaction to this treatment is to focus on its disorderliness, its rupturing of the natural bond between guest and host:

> Good my friends, consider
> You are my guests. Do me no foul play, friends.
>
> (28–9)
>
> I am your host.
> With robbers' hands my hospitable favours
> You should not ruffle thus.   (37–9)

His oppressors' intentions are of course much more vicious than Gloucester at first realises, beginning with the intention to offer 'the form of justice' (24) in place of true justice. Their questioning of Gloucester is not aimed at discovering truth, but is from the outset a knowingly fake trial designed to provide the framework for the vicious acts of supposed punishment that follow. In form it recalls not only the mock-trial of the previous scene, where Lear arraigns his absent daughters, genuinely seeking to find the answer to the question whether there is 'any cause in nature' that makes hard hearts (3.6.71), but also the opening trial of love. The concern with injustice and the failure of the supposed institutions of justice runs right through the play. As Bond comments in the introduction to his own *Lear*, 'Law and order is one of the steps taken to maintain injustice'.[8]

Gloucester's form of speech changes as he begins to realise that there is no hope for justice here, only vicious oppression; and his first indication of anger in answering the question why he sent the King to Dover is an ironic anticipation of what is to come for him:

> Because I would not see thy cruel nails
> Pluck out his poor old eyes, nor thy fierce sister
> In his anointed flesh rash boarish fangs.
>
> (53–5)

His answer picks up on Goneril's first words in this scene and provokes the astounding act of cruelty that follows, as Cornwall actually plucks out Gloucester's eye with his own hands; but this outrage in turn provokes the intervention that forces the audience to see humanity co-existing with inhumanity. The courage of Cornwall's servant in intervening is as astonishing as his master's cruelty, the more so precisely because this master is so cruel that he can be expected to turn all his brutality on an interfering servant who dares to lecture him on his duty:

> Hold your hand, my lord.
> I have served ever since I was a child,
> But better service have I never done you
> Than now to bid you hold.   (69–72)

Regan turns on the servant even before Cornwall: 'How now, you dog!' (72); and her term of abuse takes up a strand of imagery which dominates both this play and *Timon of Athens* before it, bringing together here ongoing concerns with injustice and random cruelty. Dogs in *Lear* become symbolic of figures who either inflict cruelty ('dog-hearted daughters' (4.3.45)) or suffer it ('Why, madam, if I were your father's dog / You could not use me so' (2.2.127–8)) and also figures of jumped-up authority ('a dog's obeyed in office' (4.6.151–2)).[9] They are present too by implication in Gloucester's own statement of resignation earlier in this scene, 'I am tied to th' stake, and I must stand the course' (51), since bearbaiting involved the savaging of a fettered bear by dogs. Cornwall, however, expresses his outrage in feudal terms: 'My villain!' (75; the term originally meant 'serf'). He is shocked that a mere servant should reverse the social order by stepping out of line in this way. The reversal of social hierarchy here echoes the care Lear's servants take for their liege lord, who should take care of them, in the preceding scenes. It also anticipates the healing reversal in which Lear kneels to Cordelia, instead of expecting her to kneel to him (4.7.57).

The events of this scene follow pell-mell: the servant wounds Cornwall; Regan kills the servant; Cornwall takes out Gloucester's other eye; and Regan thrusts him out of his own castle to 'smell / His way to Dover' (90–1). But before he is cast out, Gloucester, newly blind, is made to see the truth he has hitherto failed to see: that Edgar, not Edmund, is the son who loves him. Astoundingly, even at this height of suffering, Gloucester addresses the gods as 'kind' in asking their forgiveness (89). Both Gloucester's blindness and the address to the gods echo the Lear plot. When Lear insists on blindly following through his banishment of Cordelia, Kent begs him to 'See better, Lear, and let me still remain / The true blank of thine eye'; and when Lear begins to swear by the god Apollo in his rage at Kent's intervention, Kent tells him: 'thou swearest thy gods in vain' (1.1.148–50). His warning is prophetic. The gods will seem to absent themselves from any response to the events that follow. Both Lear and Gloucester pursue the paths of blindness until they are made to see, Lear gradually and Gloucester abruptly. (Lear's path towards vision begins after Goneril has tried to cut his retinue. As the Fool jokes pointedly about daughters and foolish men, Lear cuts across his wit with a shaft of plainness: 'I did her wrong' (1.5.23).)

The scene ends with the choric commentary of Cornwall's two remaining servants underlining the wickedness of Cornwall and the monstrosity of Regan and looking, as Kent and the Fool have done with Lear, to respond to Gloucester's most basic needs: one goes to fetch Poor Tom to lead him, while the other goes for 'flax and whites of eggs / To apply to his bleeding face' (103–4). Both actions are crucial, but appear only in the Quarto text: they keep Gloucester alive, they reunite him unknowingly with Edgar and they make possible Edgar's rescue of Gloucester from despair. Thus three anonymous servants change the course of the play from a nadir where all is 'dark and comfortless' (3.7.82) to a point where fathers can be reunited with the children they have wronged. Film versions such as Peter Brook's (1971), that follow the Folio in omitting the humane close of this scene, present a much bleaker picture than the Quarto does. Kurosawa's *Ran*, by contrast, substitutes an emblematic moment of tenderness much earlier for this particular narrative detail, having the son of Hidetora (Lear) cut branches from the only visible tree in a wide empty landscape to provide shade for Hidetora when he falls asleep in the open sun.[10]

Vision

How far there is room for optimism in the play, however, is not as straightforward as the upward movement at the end of this scene suggests. *Lear* is much more mixed in its form than to allow any single trajectory to dominate. Often compared with *As You Like It*, which presents a similar move away from the sophistication of the court to the simplicity of the forest, but in comic form, *Lear* complicates its quasi-pastoral with anti-pastoral forms of suffering that are not easily resolved. *Titus Andronicus* and *Timon of Athens*, as we have seen, also present scenes in a 'green world' where the action is far from Utopian. Indeed, some of the worst atrocities in *Titus* take place in the forest. The outdoor scenes in the middle of *Lear* are not set in a green wood, even one occasionally visited by bad weather, as in *As You Like It* (which also incorporates its own anti-pastoral element); they suggest a hostile location, exposed to the worst of the storm, and they represent the encounter that Lear most fears: with madness.[11]

Even those who care for him are not always comforting. The Fool, 'who labours to outjest / His heart-struck injuries' (3.1.16–17) in the storm, jests from the start with a bitterness designed to make Lear see his folly clearly, not to distance him from his pain. Some of the Fool's bitterness, however, was aimed at a different King, one outside the fiction and viewing it, and the absence from the Folio text of such gibes as the one against monopolies (1.4.142–5), was almost certainly due to censorship. His presence, however, though markedly different in each text, is central in both to the barbed tone of the play, with its characteristically painful mix of wit and suffering; and it is hardly surprising that Nahum Tate's pastoral-comic rewriting of the play, which held the stage for about a hundred and fifty years, chose to dispense with the Fool altogether.[12] Tate's more anodyne version, however, is indicative of how unbearable the experience of Shakespeare's *King Lear* seemed in the late seventeenth and eighteenth centuries. Samuel Johnson famously preferred Tate's adaptation, in which Lear and Gloucester survive and Cordelia marries Edgar, to Shakespeare's refusal to provide poetic justice. Edward Bond, Jan Kott and Peter Brook, by contrast, represented a late twentieth-century structure of feeling in focusing more harshly on the play's pain almost to the exclusion of its moments of more positive vision. For Bond, indeed, Shakespeare's play is not cruel enough, and his own rewriting of it heightens the cruelty.

The real power, and also the difficulty, of the play lie in the tension between its positive and negative poles. The scene selected above as core shows the puzzle clearly: what kind of meaning or coherence is there in a world where some human beings revel in torturing and maiming one another while others risk their own lives to rescue them? And similar tensions underpin the end of the play equally starkly. Lear, reunited with Cordelia, foresees a utopian freedom in imprisonment:

> Come, let's away to prison.
> We two alone will sing like birds i' th' cage.
> When thou dost ask me blessing, I'll kneel down
> And ask of thee forgiveness; so we'll live,
> And pray, and sing, and tell old tales, and laugh
> At gilded butterflies, and hear poor rogues

> Talk of court news, and we'll talk with them too,
> Who loses and who wins, who's in, who's out,
> And take upon's the mystery of things
> As if we were God's spies; and we'll wear out
> In a walled prison packs and sects of great ones
> That ebb and flow by th' moon.   (5.3.8–19)

The sheer length of the speech is important. Its rhythms, its lyrical mode and its cumulative, flowing syntax give symbolic weight to the vision it expresses; and its easy dismissal of court intrigues as trivial and transitory, its valuing of telling old tales and laughing together about 'who's in, who's out', are highly persuasive. As so often, the play moves from the political to the personal.

But the move itself is open to question. Such optimism is readable as either a moment of insight or as the naïve hope of an old man whose state of mind is dubious; and the events of the play's final scenes continue to offer and withdraw hope from moment to moment. Gloucester's conversion from despair to hope parallels Lear's brief vision of happiness in prison and is equally short-lived. Falsely persuaded by Edgar that the gods have rescued him from certain death, he vows to bear affliction to the limit, but is immediately tempted to despair again by finding Lear mad (4.6.206–8). Edgar postpones the revelation of his identity to Gloucester until the point where Gloucester's 'flawed heart', too weak to endure the shock, ''Twixt two extremes of passion, joy and grief, / Burst[s] smilingly' (5.3.190–3). Kent similarly finds the 'strings of life' cracking when he recounts 'the most piteous tale of Lear and him' (5.3.210, 208).[13]

Edmund, unlike Iago, finds in himself the need to do some good before he dies, 'Despite of mine own nature' (5.3.237), but his efforts to recall the order to kill Lear and Cordelia come too late for Cordelia. As Lear enters with Cordelia in his arms, the vision to which it prompts Kent, Edgar and Albany is as far from Lear's earlier vision of himself and Cordelia in each other's arms in prison as it could be:

> KENT
>   Is this the promised end?
>
> EDGAR
> Or image of that horror?
>
> ALBANY
>   Fall and cease.
>   (5.3.256–7)

Lear's fleeting hope that Cordelia lives is poignantly set between this moment of apocalyptic despair in the onlookers and Kent's reiteration of that hopelessness:

'All's cheerless, dark, and deadly' (5.3.282). The utterance recalls Gloucester's 'All dark and comfortless' (3.7.82), but in place of the redeeming moment of the servant's loyalty which calls that vision into question, there is Lear's realisation that Cordelia is truly dead, and his own agony, represented in the Quarto text by the repeated 'O, O, O, O', expressing pain beyond words (5.3.301). (In the Folio text this becomes another moment of vain hope that Cordelia lives. If this was Shakespeare revising, he seems to hover over how long to prolong the alternation between hope and despair in these final moments.) The play closes with the characteristic restoration of order, but its tone is crushed and tired:

> ALBANY
> The weight of this sad time we must obey,
> Speak what we feel, not what we ought to say.
> The oldest hath borne most; we that are young
> Shall never see so much, nor live so long.[14]
>   (5.3.315–18)

The play is extraordinarily daring in its combination of tragic and comic strands. A comic resolution, common to both the source-play and Tate's later adaptation, is within a hair's breadth before it is withdrawn. The effect is wholly different from the ending of *Timon*, where the hero refuses to acknowledge the more positive aspect of humanity, chides his steward for preventing him from hating all mankind and seeks the death he finds. In *Lear* characters want to find and create reasons for hope. Not one servant but three show themselves loyal; loving children continue to love their fathers after they are rejected; even the self-proclaimed villain repents. But as to whether the play celebrates hope more strongly than it urges despair, the strands will not separate. Hope is repeatedly betrayed by reasons for despair, and despair is continually redeemed by grounds for hope. Edgar, reflecting on the pain of the struggle to hold on to life, finds the bitterness of life inseparable from its sweetness, the one almost a consequence of the other:

> O our lives' sweetness,
> That we the pain of death would hourly die
> Rather than die at once.   (5.3.178–80)

The spectators are shown, as Edgar is, the terrible sweetness of life made sweeter by the knowledge and certainty of death.

Chapter 9

Macbeth

Macbeth is the only one of Shakespeare's tragedies for which an eyewitness report of a performance at the Globe survives. Simon Forman, a physician and astrologer, interested in magic and the occult, described a performance of the play in April 1611 in his *Book of Plays*.[1] The play was probably completed and performed, however, both at the Globe and at court, in 1606. It may well have formed part of the entertainments James I laid on that summer for the visit of his brother-in-law, King Christian of Denmark. The King's Men were paid for three performances of unnamed plays during that period, one at Hampton Court and two at Greenwich. As with *Lear*, *Macbeth* is a highly topical play, closely attuned to its political moment, and its references to equivocation (notably in the Porter scene, 2.3), certainly suggest a date following Father Henry Garnet's trial in connection with the Gunpowder Plot on 28 March 1606. (Garnet was hanged on 3 May.)[2] It also spoke directly to several of the King's other interests and concerns, including witchcraft (he had published a book on the subject, *Demonology*, in 1597), his own ancestry and touching for the 'King's evil' (scrofula). Kenneth Muir argues that we should not assume that these subjects were dragged into the play to please and flatter James, but it is difficult to conclude that their insertion was anything other than pointed in this way.[3]

Revision, if not collaboration, is again a question with regard to this play. Scholars have long known that two of the witches' songs recur in Middleton's play *The Witch* (of uncertain date, but probably later than *Macbeth*). The usual assumption is that the songs were written by Middleton and inserted into *Macbeth* at some date after its first composition, and some critics also believe that the Hecate scenes in which the songs appear, 3.4 and part of 4.1, were also written by Middleton or another reviser. None of this would have been unusual in the Jacobean theatre, where writers frequently revised one another's work to bring its appeal up to date. There has simply been a tendency to occlude this knowledge when thinking about Shakespeare.

Ghosts and witches

Most of Simon Forman's fairly full account of *Macbeth* retells the story, but he is particularly struck by the opening scenes, with the witches' prophecies, and by three very visual moments, all Shakespeare's additions to the source material of Holinshed's *Chronicles*:

> And when Macbeth had murdered the king, the blood on his hands could not be washed off by any means, nor from his wife's hands, which handled the bloody daggers in hiding them, by which means they became much amazed and affronted . . .
>
> [Macbeth] began to speak of noble Banquo, and to wish that he were there. And as he thus did, standing up to drink a carouse to him, the ghost of Banquo came and sat down in his chair behind him. And he, turning about to sit down again, saw the ghost of Banquo, which fronted him so, that he fell into a great passion of fear and fury, uttering many words about his murder . . .
>
> Observe also how Macbeth's queen did rise in the night in her sleep, and walked and talked and confessed all, and the doctor noted her words.
>
> Simon Forman, *Book of Plays and Notes Thereof* (1611)

The opening scene of *Macbeth* is totally unlike the increasingly realistic openings that have marked the tragedies immediately preceding it, which typically open in mid-conversation. (*Timon*, with its allegorical bent, is somewhat different, but even so, it opens with a relatively colloquial exchange.) With its thunder and lightning and its three witches speaking in riddling rhyme, *Macbeth* clearly marks a new departure and visibly sets out to depict a world apart from the very human worlds that have dominated *Othello* and *King Lear*.

The appearance of the Ghost in *Julius Caesar* represents a brief and rather surprising intrusion into the affairs of men. Even *Hamlet*, despite its Ghost, depicts a world in which the Ghost seems intrusive, a restless spirit straining to intervene in a world where the living seem preoccupied by everyday business and have to be reminded of the reality of the spirit world. In *Macbeth*, by contrast, the first thing we see is the witches, which gives them a kind of prior reality. An audience is not in a position to doubt the external reality of figures who appear first in the play, before any character from whose mind they might otherwise have sprung is presented. Though their substantiality is evident, however, their status is not. Holinshed says that opinion was divided: 'these women were either the weird sisters, that is (as ye would say) the goddesses of destiny, or else some nymphs or fairies, endued with knowledge of prophecy by their necromantical science'.[4] Shakespeare leaves their status unresolved.

The stage directions call them 'witches' and they can vanish at will; they call themselves 'the Weird Sisters' (the word 'weird' meaning 'fate' or 'destiny'); and Banquo's puzzlement on first seeing them draws attention to their uncertain status:

> What are these,
> So wither'd and so wild in their attire,
> That look not like th' inhabitants o' th' earth,
> And yet are on't? Live you? or are you aught
> That man may question?   (1.3.39–43)

But it is not clear that responsibility for the wicked deeds of the play falls on them.

Macbeth is first presented to us through the witches' speech, rather than the other way round, and both we and they know that they will meet with him before he knows it. Thus, when his first line ('So foul and fair a day I have not seen' (1.3.38)) echoes the lines the witches chant in unison to close the first scene ('Fair is foul, and foul is fair: / Hover through the fog and filthy air' (1.1.11–12)), the effect is to position Macbeth within the framework of the witches' world rather than in free and voluntary interaction with it. The question of what kind of world Macbeth occupies and what kind of agency he has within it is thus raised straight away, and replayed in fluid and ambiguous ways thereafter. Holinshed's account of events depicts Macbeth as 'encouraged' but not compelled to kill the King, and his wife as a stronger force than the weird sisters: 'The words of the three sisters . . . greatly encouraged him hereunto, but specially his wife lay sore upon him to attempt the thing, as she that was very ambitious, burning in unquenchable desire to bear the name of a queen.'[5] (This is Holinshed's only reference to Lady Macbeth, who is otherwise entirely Shakespeare's invention.) Shakespeare teases out these influences in far more detail and sets them alongside the tormented inner world of Macbeth's soliloquies, in which his own responsibility for his actions is seen developing.

The play's early scenes repeatedly signal Macbeth's occupation of two worlds simultaneously, his half-absence from the world of practical affairs. (The man of action is inherent in the Captain's description of Macbeth on the battlefield in 1.2, but the audience does not encounter Macbeth directly before he meets the witches in 1.3.) The word 'rapt', meaning 'transported' or 'enchanted', from the Latin *raptus* ('seized') is used several times over to reiterate the way the witches and the thoughts they inspire transport him almost literally into another world:

BANQUO
My noble partner
You greet with present grace, and great prediction
Of noble having, and of royal hope,
That he seems rapt withal.   (1.3.54–7)

BANQUO
Look, how our partner's rapt.
(1.3.143)

LADY MACBETH
[reading from Macbeth's letter to her]
'When I burn'd in desire to question them further, they made themselves
air, into which they vanish'd. Whiles I stood rapt in the wonder of it, came
missives from the King, who all-hail'd me, 'Thane of Cawdor'; by which
title, before, these Weird Sisters saluted me.'   (1.5.3–9)

The first of these comments on Macbeth's state immediately follows the witches'
prophecy, which Banquo observes causes Macbeth to 'start, and seem to fear /
Things that do sound so fair' (1.3.51–2). This seems to hint that the prophecies take up thoughts already present in Macbeth's mind rather than implant
them for the first time. The aside represents an emblematic mode of speech
for Macbeth, signifying the distance between the worlds within and without
him. Banquo's second comment is made in the company of Rosse and Angus,
following Macbeth's lengthy soliloquy in response to the prophecies, a speech
which shows the thought of murder already in Macbeth's mind, though 'yet . . .
but fantastical', and calls attention to the rift between the two worlds he is hence
to occupy: 'nothing is, but what is not' (1.3.139, 142).

From the point where Macbeth returns to his wife and begins to plot the
murder as a reality, his struggle to maintain an existence across two worlds is
made worse by the need for conscious craft and deceit. Where before he was
unconsciously 'rapt' by the intrusion of unwelcome imaginings, now he must
voluntarily distance himself from the world of everyday reality by masking
his true intentions. He must 'look like th'innocent flower, / But be the serpent under't' (1.5.64–5); 'False face must hide what the false heart doth know'
(1.7.83). The first utterance, characteristically, is Lady Macbeth's command;
the second, which is also the closing line of a scene, is Macbeth's statement
of resolve. But Macbeth, at least at first, is to find it impossible to maintain a
separation between the worlds he occupies. The one bleeds into the other in
ways beyond conscious control. The first sign is the appearance of the dagger.
Unlike the witches, who have material substance on stage, the dagger is clearly

marked by Macbeth's speech as insubstantial, invisible to the audience, 'A dagger of the mind, a false creation, / Proceeding from the heat-oppressed brain' (2.1.38–9). Its 'appearance' is a powerful marker of the invasive intensity of Macbeth's inner world. A German visitor to one of Garrick's performances in the role reported that 'a certain foreigner in his box, though understanding not a word of English, was so moved by Garrick's mere gesture in reaching out for the imaginary dagger . . . that he collapsed in a swoon'.[6]

A second sign is his inability, as he performs the murder, to say 'Amen' in response to hearing Duncan's son cry out 'God bless us!' as he sleeps (2.2.26–32). A third is the voice that cries out to him in his imagination that he himself will sleep no more (2.2.34–42); and a fourth is perhaps the one that Forman notes, the inability to wash off the blood. (It is not clear from the extant text that Macbeth is actually trying to wash his hands when he utters the fear that not 'all great Neptune's ocean' will wash the blood away (2.2.59), but Forman's account seems to indicate that such an action did take place in the Globe performance.)

The climax of these invasions of the other world is of course the appearance of Banquo's ghost. Stage directions, together with Forman's account, make clear that the Ghost was a material presence on stage, though it never speaks. It is not incontrovertibly clear, however, that it has a substantial reality beyond Macbeth's imagination, since no-one but Macbeth sees it. We have seen before, in *Hamlet*, that ghosts which do have a substantial reality can nevertheless choose before whom to make themselves visible. Hamlet's mother does not see the Ghost when it appears to Hamlet in her closet, but its earlier appearances have confirmed its substantiality (though Richard Eyre's 1980 production, with Jonathan Pryce both playing Hamlet and speaking the Ghost's lines, suggested a contrary interpretation – one at odds, in my view, with the fact that others see the Ghost before Hamlet does). *Macbeth*, by contrast, depicts a world in which the 'other world' increasingly takes possession, but where that 'other world', harnessed to Macbeth's 'fit' (3.4.20) becomes impossible to read outside Macbeth's own reading of it. The audience is not given a position from which to judge it as either a product of Macbeth's imagination or a manifestation of the supernatural.

Towards all of these invasions of another world, whether of the imagination or the supernatural, Lady Macbeth is brisk and dismissive, urging Macbeth not 'to think / So brainsickly of things' (2.2.44–5), convinced that 'A little water clears us of this deed' (2.2.65–6). She rightly recognises the Ghost as the return of the 'air-drawn dagger', 'the very painting of your fear' (3.4.60–1) and insists that 'When all's done, / You look but on a stool' (3.4.66–7). Ironically, given Macbeth's description of his own anxiety as his 'fit', Lady Macbeth calls upon the same word to explain Macbeth's extraordinary behaviour at the feast to his guests:

> Sit, worthy friends. My Lord is often thus,
> And hath been from his youth: pray you, keep seat;
> The fit is momentary; upon a thought
> He will again be well.   (3.4.52–5)

The word positions Macbeth's behaviour as a sickness, an aberration, a form of behaviour scarcely explicable other than through medical diagnosis. Yet even Lady Macbeth is to find herself susceptible to such uncontrollable manifestations of anxiety. The scene of her sleepwalking was to become one of the best-known set-pieces of Shakespearean tragic performance, and the particular triumph of the eighteenth-century actress, Sarah Siddons. Mrs Siddons, who describes the sheer terror of first immersing herself in the part, took the view that Lady Macbeth, 'having impiously delivered herself up to the excitements of hell . . . is abandoned to the guidance of the demons she has invoked'.[7] In other words, so Siddons believed, even the strong agency and will that Lady Macbeth demonstrates in the early stages of the play are lost to the other world that takes her over. The prevalence of night-scenes often noted in this play is not accidental, but linked to the various kinds of darkness it explores, from the 'simple' emblematism of darkness standing for evil to the more complex darknesses of the invisibility, insubstantiality or incomprehensibility of what is happening. *Macbeth*, like *Lear*, depicts an ultimately unreadable universe; but where, in *Lear*, it is the gods and the potential presence of any divine plan that are unknowable, in *Macbeth* the uncertain boundary between human beings and the spirit world renders humanity itself unknowable. It is unclear where free will ends and possession begins.

Deeds of violence

The darkness of Macbeth himself brings a new aspect to the tragic hero. The 'great passion of fear and fury' that Forman notes about him is tied to a Senecan intensity of focus on blood which recalls the world of *Titus Andronicus*.[8] The violent and bloody images of the play, the horses that eat each other, the mother plucking her child from the nipple to dash out its brains, the bloody child, the 'blood-bolter'd Banquo' (4.1.123), conjure up a world where this kind of interaction seems the norm, and Macbeth's soliloquies take us into the heart of what it feels like to be immersed in such violence:

> It will have blood, they say: blood will have blood:
>
> (3.4.121)

> I am in blood
> Stepp'd in so far, that, should I wade no more,
> Returning were as tedious as go o'er.
>
> (3.4.135–7)

It is as though we were taken inside the mind of a villain with the self-consciousness of a tragic hero, in order to empathise with what it is to be a man who has reached the edge of humanity. For the actor of Macbeth, '[t]he main difficulty lies in persuading audiences to identify with a downright brute', though the soliloquies give the actor extraordinary raw material with which to do that.[9] Expressionistic sets, both on stage and on film, often work to confirm the dominant presence of Macbeth's inner world by constructing the stage world as an extension of it. Kurosawa's *Throne of Blood*, with its fog-bound Cobweb Forest, shot on Mount Fuji, is perhaps the classic instance.

It is logical that *Macbeth* should reach this point after the limits to which *Lear* pushed in exploring inhuman cruelty and the concern throughout the tragedies with what it is to be a man. In this play, both of the two central protagonists are capable of inhuman cruelty; both are tormented by invasions of the imagination that speak to them of their own unnaturalness; and the degree of agency by which they reach a state of being which is barely human ('this dead butcher, and his fiend-like Queen' (5.9.35)) is left open to question. Throughout the play these two oppose one another's views of manhood. The opposition is evident even before we see them together, as Lady Macbeth, reading Macbeth's letter, expresses the fear that he is 'too full o' the milk of human kindness / To catch the nearest way' to the throne (1.5.17–18). She recasts Macbeth's reservations of conscience as fear:

> Art thou afeard
> To be the same in thine own act and valour,
> As thou art in desire?   (1.7.39–41)

and Macbeth, at this early point in the play, recognises this as a false view of manhood:

> I dare do all that may become a man;
> Who dares do more is none.
>
> (1.7.46–7)

Their relationship and their views on manhood may be compared with those of Brutus and Portia in *Julius Caesar* (chapter 4 above), where there is a partial parallel between two men wrestling with conscience and two women adopting seeming masculinity to shame their husbands. The parallel importantly and instructively breaks down in several ways: Portia, excluded from her husband's confidence, wounds herself in order to demonstrate her courage and endurance and to shame him into treating her as an equal partner. She neither knows that he is contemplating murder, nor urges him towards it. The concept of manhood she challenges is the Stoic *virtus* which, if it verges on the inhuman, does so through an excess of restraint. In *Macbeth*, by contrast, it is the female partner who verges on inhumanity by insisting that, if she had sworn as Macbeth has, to a common 'enterprise', she would have plucked her nipple from the infant smiling in her face and dashed its brains out (1.7.47–59). This concept of manhood has nothing to do with restraint and everything to do with excess: of violence.

Core scene: 4.2

The killing of Macduff's wife and children, often cut from early performances as being too painful, is expanded from the mere statement in Holinshed that 'Macbeth most cruelly caused the wife and children of Macduff, with all other whom he found in that castle, to be slain'.[10] It creates the space for several important perspectives: a brief view of the ordinary life that goes on outside the violent and hallucinatory world of Macbeth and his wife; the representation of a very different woman and a very different set of family relationships; and the intimate exploration of real fear, of what it feels like to be on the receiving end of one of Macbeth's acts of violence. The scene begins by depicting Lady Macduff's failure to understand why Macduff has fled. Commentators on the play frequently take Lady Macduff's position for the audience's; but an attentive audience knows from the previous scene that Macduff has gone to England to seek help against Macbeth from Duncan's son, Malcolm, and the King of England.[11] Like Brutus, Macduff has not confided in his wife (perhaps, in this case, to protect all concerned and maintain secrecy, as Rosse implies in suggesting it is 'wisdom' (4.2.5)); and she, unlike a proud Roman wife, concludes that he has fled out of fear. Macbeth too, at first so closely bound to his wife, has now ceased to tell her of his intentions. The murders of Banquo and Macduff are planned by Macbeth alone, and Lady Macbeth has already complained of Macbeth's increasing distance from her (3.2.8–11).

Macbeth's reign of terror, this scene shows us, brings not only death but also loss of faith. The scene opens with Lady Macduff questioning Rosse as to why her husband has fled the country; and there is a bitter irony for the audience in Lady Macduff's judgement of her husband in terms which would better fit Macbeth: 'He loves us not: / He wants the natural touch' (4.2.8–9). When Rosse assures her that her husband is 'noble, wise, judicious, and best knows / The fits o' th' season'

(4.2.16–17), the word 'fits' again recalls Macbeth, the point here being that Macbeth's fits of terror are experienced as random 'fits' of the time by those under his government. The scene shows the working out of the personal in the political realm; but it does so by showing the political as itself personal. The Scotland that has become 'Almost afraid to know itself' (4.3.165) is made real and powerful through the individual and intimate experience of one family. Lady Macduff and her children die believing their husband and father to be a traitor. One of the saddest moments of the scene is when Macduff's son asks his mother 'Was my father a traitor, mother?' and she answers: 'Ay, that he was' (4.2.44–5).

Rosse leaves because, he says, he will disgrace himself with weeping if he stays. Thus ideas of manhood are again recalled, and Rosse's humanity is implicitly contrasted with Macbeth's increasing inability to care about human suffering:

> But let the frame of things disjoint, both the worlds suffer,
> Ere we will eat our meal in fear, and sleep
> In the affliction of these terrible dreams
> That shake us nightly.   (3.2.16–19)

Womanhood is similarly explored through the implicit contrast between Lady Macduff's care for her children and Lady Macbeth's expressed willingness to dash her child's brains out. The son's concern for his mother, and his childish attempts to keep her spirits up, similarly represent an image of deep family love inaccessible to either Macbeth or his wife, and his naïve questions and opinions cast a harsh light on the political state of the nation in which this family finds itself:

SON
And must they all be hang'd that swear and lie?

LADY MACDUFF
Every one.

SON
Who must hang them?

LADY MACDUFF
Why, the honest men.

SON
Then the liars and swearers are fools; for there are liars and swearers enow
to beat the honest men and hang up them.   (51–7)

Self-evidently, though this 'Poor prattler' (63) cannot know it, Scotland has become a nation where the liars and swearers do indeed beat and hang the honest men.

The scene exploits the pathos of the situation as Lady Macduff and her son offer such hopeless resistance as they can to the murderers and the son seeks to protect his mother; but Shakespeare knew when to stop, cutting the scene off as the son dies, calling out to his mother to run away. Some reminder of the potential strength of family love is an important intervention in the relentlessly dark world of the Macbeths, which is otherwise almost the only world the audience is allowed to occupy.

Yet the scene that follows allows one further perspective on the world outside Macbeth's castle, one that picks up the thread of this scene and the ongoing consideration, over several scenes, of manhood. It is the scene where Macduff meets with Malcolm, aiming to persuade him to return to Scotland to challenge Macbeth for the throne. Malcolm's testing of Macduff reveals him as a man of integrity before he then receives, and must react to, news of the murder of his family. Macduff's first response is to withdraw silently into himself. As Malcolm urges him to 'Give sorrow words' (4.3.209), his shocked questions at first simply echo Rosse's news: 'My children too? . . . My wife kill'd too?' (4.3.211, 213). But as his shock gives way to passion, Malcolm chides him: 'Dispute it like a man', and his response forms an important corrective to the notions of manhood which preoccupy Macbeth and his wife:

> I shall do so;
> But I must also feel it as a man:
> I cannot but remember such things were,
> That were most precious to me.
>
> (4.3.220–3)

His insistence on the need to feel as a man takes further Macbeth's opposition to his wife's understanding of manhood as wholly defined by deeds of violence. The scene makes clear that Macduff does not shrink from necessary violence, and as he turns his grief into a determination to kill Macbeth, Malcolm is satisfied that 'This tune goes manly' (4.3.235). But the audience has felt the force of Macduff's demonstration that a real man must feel human emotion as well as act with resolution. Macbeth, increasingly isolated by his acts of violence, no longer has a wife or friends in any true sense. On the contrary, he 'keep[s] a servant fee'd' to spy in the houses of all those he once called friends (3.4.131). The implication for his manhood is clear.[12]

Signifying nothing

What, then, is tragic about this play? The tragedy of Lear, and to some extent Timon, are tragedies of men who experience inhumanity in those around them. They behave foolishly, even badly, but not monstrously. Yet there is no denying that Macbeth does behave monstrously. Indeed many of Shakespeare's alterations to his source were designed to emphasise his guilt. The question then follows: can a monster be a tragic hero? It may be that Shakespeare wrote the play precisely in order to test the limits of tragedy with this question. What he does is to draw the audience into Macbeth's inner world so closely that they cannot help but feel what it is like to be him. Despite the invitation in 4.2 to feel what it is like to be Macbeth's victim, the overwhelmingly dominant perspective is Macbeth's and the most powerful mechanism by which this perspective is produced is the soliloquy. The intensity with which the play focuses on Macbeth's inner world is largely created by packing several long and densely experienced soliloquies, together with numerous shorter asides, into an abnormally brief space of time. (*Macbeth*, at around 2100 lines, is one of Shakespeare's shortest plays.)[13]

The real effect of these is cumulative, and the length and rhythm of each meditation is part of its characteristic tenor, but something of Macbeth's inner world can be evoked by selecting a few moments:

> Present fears
> Are less than horrible imaginings;
> (1.3.137–8)

> Stars, hide your fires!
> Let not light see my black and deep desires;
> (1.4.50–1)

> If it were done, when 'tis done, then 'twere well
> It were done quickly;   (1.7.1–2)

> Is this a dagger, which I see before me,
> The handle toward my hand?
> (2.1.33–4)

> Methought, I heard a voice cry, 'Sleep no more!
> Macbeth does murther Sleep';   (2.2.34–5)

> O! full of scorpions is my mind, dear wife!
> (3.2.36)

> I have supp'd full with horrors:
> Direness, familiar to my slaughterous thoughts,
> Cannot once start me.   (5.5.13–15)

But the most memorable soliloquies, and those which begin to signal where the tragedy of the play lies, are the late ones, when Macbeth begins to take stock of what he has lost:

> I have liv'd long enough: my way of life
> Is fall'n into the sere, the yellow leaf;
> And that which should accompany old age,
> As honour, love, obedience, troops of friends,
> I must not look to have. (5.3.22–6)

The feeling of a life wasted rather than fulfilled is stronger here than even in any of the most agonised moments of *Lear*. Part of the tragedy of Lear is to rediscover love and joy before losing them. Macbeth, by contrast, finds himself so empty of feeling that even the death of the one person to whom he has seemed close cannot touch him. The cry of women offstage, mourning Lady Macbeth, is set against Macbeth's own aridity of response:

> She should have died hereafter:
> There would have been a time for such a word.
>   (5.5.17–18)

The suffering of the speech that follows has in it nothing so intense as agony, only a deeply tired sense of futility, of a life emptied of meaning. The character is given lines that reduce him to a mere caricature of the actor who plays him:

> Life's but a walking shadow; a poor player,
> That struts and frets his hour upon the stage,
> And then is heard no more: it is a tale
> Told by an idiot, full of sound and fury,
> Signifying nothing. (5.5.24–8)

Instances of metatheatrical and metanarrative awareness, and the difference between them, are discussed in relation to several plays above (see esp. pp. 62–3; cf pp. 37–8, 40–2, 75–6, 88). Moments in which the tragic hero can see the shape of his story can give both the character and the play a sense of closure and fulfilment. For Macbeth, however, the failure to find narrative coherence in his own life signals a climax of desperation.[14] At the same time, nevertheless, it is the capacity for despair that keeps him human and allows the play to achieve the status of tragedy. Unlike Timon, who seeks to deny the full awareness of what it is to be human that the play sets before him, Macbeth confronts it squarely. His tragedy is to know so clearly how he has failed as a man.

Chapter 10

Antony and Cleopatra

Antony and Cleopatra was probably completed by the end of 1606 and perhaps performed at court over Christmas of that year. When it was first performed at the Globe remains uncertain, since the public theatres remained closed for long periods in 1607 as a result of plague. It is possible, though not certain, however, that Samuel Daniel was influenced by having seen a production of Shakespeare's *Antony and Cleopatra* in writing his own *Cleopatra* (1607), which describes Cleopatra raising Antony to the monument thus:

> She draws him up in rolls of taffeta
> T'a window at the top
> . . .
>
> There Charmion, and poor Eras, two weak maids
> Foretir'd with watching, and their mistress' care,
> Tugg'd at the pulley, having n'other aids,
> And up they hoise [hoisted] the swooning body there
> Of pale Antonius, show'ring out his blood
> On th'underlookers, which there gazing stood.[1]

The detail of this description, as Joan Rees points out, comes neither from Plutarch nor from Shakespeare's text, but perhaps hints at a visual memory of this difficult scene (4.15) in performance.

Like *Timon of Athens* and *Julius Caesar*, *Antony and Cleopatra* returns to Plutarch for its source material, focusing on the figure of Antony, who not only appears in more than one of Plutarch's *Lives*, and whose own life was already a source for *Timon*, but whom Shakespeare had already dramatised once in *Julius Caesar*. And like all the tragedies from *Timon* onwards, it seems to resonate with topical allusion, especially to court matters. James I's liking for parallels drawn between himself and the Emperor Augustus (the later title of Octavius Caesar in the play) was well known, and, at a more critical level, the extravagance of Antony and Cleopatra may have seemed to contemporary audiences reminiscent of the kind of spending for which the Jacobean court had become notorious. Even more risky (and for that reason more dubious),

126

are the parallels some critics have drawn between the debauchery and public display of sexuality in the play and James' own excesses in these respects.[2] One aspect of these parallels that would have protected Shakespeare and the King's Men from seeming to criticise the King, however, is that they are in conflict with each other. If James is figured in the austere Octavius, they could have argued, he can scarcely also be figured in the unrestrained Antony. Whether he could or not, of course, would have been a question for contemporary audiences.

Like *Romeo and Juliet* and *Othello*, the play's central subject is love; and, like the first of these, its title emphasises two protagonists rather than one. Imagining the non-existent tragedy of *Othello and Desdemona* highlights the difference between tragedies concentrating on a single protagonist and those dividing the centre of interest between two. Yet the differences between *Antony and Cleopatra* and *Romeo and Juliet* are as marked as those between *Antony and Cleopatra* and *Othello*. Whereas Romeo and Juliet die in one another's arms in a death that brings them physically together at the close of the play, Antony dies in Act 4 of this play, leaving Cleopatra's death to absorb the whole of the final act.[3] And in giving a woman the final and climactic death, the play marks itself out as unique in Shakespeare's tragic canon.

Competition

One way in which we might formulate the difference between *Romeo and Juliet* and *Antony and Cleopatra* is to say that where the first two lovers complete each other, the second two compete with each other. That competitiveness is immediately heard in their opening exchange, with its oppositional alternation of complete lines:

> CLEOPATRA
> If it be love indeed, tell me how much.
>
> MARK ANTONY
> There's beggary in the love that can be reckoned.
>
> CLEOPATRA
> I'll set a bourn how far to be beloved.
>
> MARK ANTONY
> Then must thou needs find out new heaven, new earth.
>
> (1.1.14–17)

The underlying framework of the exchange is economic: the talk is of whether or how their love can be measured and the mode of discourse strives to match one grandiose statement with another. The framing economic conceit seems to anchor their love in a hard-headed, material and ruthless environment, even as it claims to supersede it with talk of new worlds.

The exchange is also, importantly and symptomatically, public. The lovers enter with Cleopatra's train of ladies and eunuchs, and the words they utter are high rhetoric for public consumption. Unlike Romeo and Juliet, who are shown creating private space together for their first exchange even within the public space of a masked ball, or Othello and Desdemona, whose private moments together before the play opens have allowed their love to develop to the point of elopement before anyone else seems to notice it, Antony and Cleopatra are characteristically depicted displaying their love before an ever-present public. The declaration of that love is self-conscious and monumentalising even from the start

> MARK ANTONY
> Let Rome in Tiber melt, and the wide arch
> Of the ranged empire fall! Here is my space!
> Kingdoms are clay! Our dungy earth alike
> Feeds beast as man. The nobleness of life
> Is to do thus, when such a mutual pair
> And such a twain can do't, in which I bind,
> On pain of punishment, the world to weet [acknowledge]
> We stand up peerless.   (1.1.34–41)

John Wilders' punctuation of this stretch of text with repeated exclamation marks calls attention to its audible self-celebration, its conscious construction of speech as self-contained nuggets. Antony seeks to model the moment-by-moment behaviour of himself and Cleopatra as a sequence of symbolic and universalising acts ('thus' may script a single transient embrace but also points to everything their love and life together represents); he formalises and distances them in the third person as 'such a mutal pair . . . such a twain'; and their very standing in the space is held still for contemplation as an emblematic tableau: 'We stand up peerless'. From the start they speak not as two people who happen to love each other, but as two figures already aware of themselves as great and historic lovers. They construct themselves and each other as performers in an epic at least, if not yet a tragedy, from the start. And it is an epic in which each strives to outdo the other.

Such competitiveness is more frequently depicted in Shakespearean tragedy as a male-male interaction. It was particularly marked in the earlier Roman play, *Julius Caesar* (see p. 61 above); it is also a prominent feature of the relationship between Antony and Octavius in *Antony and Cleopatra*; and is to dominate

Coriolanus. Roman male identity, as Shakespeare constructs it, is powerfully agonistic. War is almost a condition of being for this kind of virility, and at times the figuration of war as a rivalry between aspiring alpha males is almost absurd. The hubristic folly to which such rivalry can lead is evident in the way Antony reaches the catastrophic decision to fight by sea, which is to be his downfall:

> ANTONY
>   Canidius, we
> Will fight with him by sea.
>
> CLEOPATRA
>   By sea – what else?
>
> CANIDIUS
> Why will my lord do so?
>
> MARK ANTONY
>   For that he dares us to't.
>   (3.7.27–9)

The die is cast because Antony will not refuse Caesar's dare. Yet, as Enobarbus and Canidius are quick to point out, Caesar knows when to refuse a dare, having already refused Antony's suggestion, simultaneously heroic and absurd, of resolving the hostilities by single combat.

The limits to which Caesar will go in displaying manhood are restrained by policy. Stoic *virtus*, as discussed in the chapters on *Julius Caesar* and *Macbeth*, is characterised by excessive restraint. Lack of restraint, by contrast, is Antony's defining characteristic, as it was Timon's; both share the same quality, the same lack of measure, which can be manifested as liberality or prodigality, as noble magnanimity or riotous excess. The point of origin for this double-sided discourse is Plutarch, who emphasises throughout the paradox that is Antony, and describes even his mode of speech as characterised, like his behaviour, by its excess:

> He used a manner of phrase in his speech, called Asiatic, which carried
> the best grace and estimation at that time, and was much like to his
> manners and life: for it was full of ostentation, foolish bravery, and vain
> ambition.[4]

Yet the paradox of Antony includes the capacity to be a great soldier as well as a great lover. Though Antony is no Stoic, he is capable of enduring more privation than any of his competitors, and even Caesar cannot withhold his praise of a man who, when not wasting his energy on 'lascivious wassails', has been known to

> drink
> The stale of horses, and the gilded puddle
> Which beasts would cough at.
>   (1.4.57, 62–4)

Where Antony differs from Octavius, from full Romanness and the Stoic heroism of *Julius Caesar*, is in not putting his honour first. In giving a woman such a dominant place in his heart and life (as Brutus will not, even in response to Portia's rebuke), he willingly, or at least knowingly, sacrifices his honour and brings almost unspeakable shame upon himself.

> I never saw an action of such shame.
> Experience, manhood, honour, ne'er before
> Did violate so itself.   (3.10.22–4)

This is Scarus' response to Antony's flight from the sea-battle of Actium; and though Antony himself expresses a similar intensity of feeling about his shame immediately afterwards (3.11.1–2), by the end of this same scene he is claiming that one tear of Cleopatra's 'rates / All that is won and lost' and one kiss of hers repays his own loss (3.11.69–71). It is not just individuals who compete with each other in this play, but spheres of action: love and war, Egypt and Rome, the world of women and the world of men.

Conflicting worlds

An alternative, but complementary, formulation to the one which began the previous section would be to suggest that where *Romeo and Juliet* uses symmetries and parallelism to suggest a unified perspective on the love it depicts, *Antony and Cleopatra* uses antitheses and ironic parallelism to suggest conflicting perspectives on the love it depicts. Though the easy response is to note, as above, the contrast between Egypt and Rome, the tensions in the play are much more paradoxical than that, and the interest of the play lies in the crossover between all that seems oppositional in each of these designations. Indeed, if Shakespeare was drawn in *Macbeth* to the challenge of how far a human being could become monstrous and remain the centre of tragedy, he may here have been drawn by the challenge of how paradoxical two individuals and the relationship between them could be within the frame of tragedy.

We have already seen that paradox is central to Plutarch's account of Antony; and it is also the case that he presents Cleopatra's charm as paradoxical, emphasising that 'her beauty . . . was not so passing [surpassing] . . . nor yet such as upon present [immediate] view did enamour men with her: but so sweet was her company and conversation, that a man could not possibly but be taken'.[5] Shakespeare represents this paradox through the mixture of reactions to Cleopatra, ranging from insult and scorn ('gipsy' (1.1.9), 'strumpet' (1.1.13), 'Eygptian dish' (2.6.128)) to stunned admiration ('The barge she sat in . . .' (2.2.201–28), a speech constituting one of Shakespeare's most extensive and direct debts to Plutarch). Perhaps most central to the impression of Cleopatra that the play creates is a speech not directly about her at all, but ostensibly about crocodiles:

> LEPIDUS
> What manner o' thing is your crocodile?
>
> MARK ANTONY
> It is shaped, sir, like itself, and it is as broad as it hath breadth. It is just so high as it is, and moves with its own organs. It lives by that which nourisheth it, and the elements once out of it, it transmigrates.
>
> LEPIDUS
> What colour is it of?
>
> MARK ANTONY
> Of it own colour too.
>
> LEPIDUS
> 'Tis a strange serpent.
>
> MARK ANTONY
> 'Tis so. And the tears of it are wet.   (2.7.41–50)

The force of 'your' in Lepidus' question is not personal; it merely means 'what kind of thing is a crocodile, then?' But as Antony's answer continues it becomes clear that he is talking about a creature that is like Cleopatra: self-defining and yet indefinable, infinitely flexible, capable of transmigration and yet very much itself.

That emphasis on transmigration is part of an ongoing emphasis on a capacity for transformation within both Antony and Cleopatra. The open-ing speech of the play is all about how Cleopatra transforms Antony from a great soldier, 'the triple pillar of the world' into 'a strumpet's fool' (1.1.12–13), and the play repeatedly shows them transforming themselves from moment to moment as the dynamics of the situation require. Their shared capacity to transform each other and themselves is also particularly figured as a crossing of gender:

> OCTAVIUS CAESAR
>   From Alexandria
> This is the news: he fishes, drinks, and wastes
> The lamps of night in revel; is not more manlike
> Than Cleopatra, nor the Queen of Ptolemy
> More womanly than he.   (1.4.3–7)

For Caesar, Antony's revelry is the sign of a man effeminised by too much time away from affairs of state and wasted with a woman. But the effeminisation goes further than even Caesar realises:

> CLEOPATRA
>   That time? O times!
> I laughed him out of patience, and that night
> I laughed him into patience, and next morn,
> Ere the ninth hour, I drunk him to his bed,
> Then put my tires and mantles on him, whilst
> I wore his sword Philippan.   (2.5.18–23)

Not only does Cleopatra drink Antony under the table, but he willingly gives up to her the very symbol of his manhood, his sword, while allowing her to dress him in her robes and headdress. The sword will return as a test of Antony's manhood, when he finds Eros more capable than himself of a truly Roman death, and fails to achieve a clean death upon his own sword.

But Antony's willingness to let go of male rigour and test out female ways of being can be viewed positively as well as negatively, and comparison with *Macbeth* is illuminating in this respect. Shakespeare had already explored a different kind of crossing of gender in *Macbeth*, an unwilling recognition on the part of both principals that Macbeth has more of the 'milk of human kindness' (1.5.17) than his wife, and that her instincts are seemingly more 'male' than his. There, the recognition is destructive: it brings out contempt on the part of Lady Macbeth for what seems to her a failure of manhood on her husband's part, and it leads Macbeth to become ever more a 'butcher' in his determination to free himself from fear without the hindrance of compassion. By comparison with Macbeth's increasing rigour, growing closer to monstrosity, Antony's flexibility can look like a very positive quality, one that allows him to encompass the best of both male and female attributes, as the opposing paeans of praise from Caesar and Cleopatra suggest (1.4.56–72 and 5.2.81–91).[6] Where Caesar sees a soldier who has endured the worst of hardships, Cleopatra sees a bounteous Colossus. And, as with Cleopatra herself, both pictures are at once true and untrue. Both Antony and Cleopatra seem endowed with the capacity to become almost anything they choose to become; but neither has any fixed essence.

From the start, we are encouraged to see that their qualities can be judged both positively and negatively, depending on the priorities of the observer and the degree of excess in their behaviour. The mid-conversation opening of the play returns to the style characteristic before *Macbeth*, and the first sentence is a criticism of Antony:

> PHILO
> Nay, but this dotage of our general's
> O'erflows the measure.   (1.1.1–2)

Not only is Philo critical, but his 'Nay, but' suggests that he may be respond-ing to a remark defending Antony. Thus immediately we are made aware of the possibility that Antony provokes a divided response. A few lines later the roles are reversed, and Philo is defending Antony against Demetrius' implied criticism:

> DEMETRIUS
> Is Caesar with Antonius prized so slight?
>
> PHILO
> Sir, sometimes, when he is not Antony,
> He comes too short of that great property
> Which still should go with Antony.
>
> (1.1.57–60)

The defence is one that highlights becoming as against being. The 'Antony' Philo values is someone that Antony can become or fail to become. And that same 'Antony' is one that Antony drops in order to become the 'Antony' that Cleopatra loves.

Repetitions of the word 'piece' suggest the combination of fragmentedness and wholeness that Antony and Cleopatra seem to represent and the conflicted mixture of admiration and contempt that they provoke. The first meaning of the word is a part or fragment; but it also contains almost the opposite meaning of a completely achieved production, as in the terms 'piece of work' or 'masterpiece'. Thus Cleopatra is 'a wonderful piece of work' (1.2.160–1) while Octavia is a 'piece of virtue' (3.2.28). Both are finished productions, but Cleopatra is 'wonderful' and undefined, while Octavia is simultaneously defined and delimited by her virtue. Antony, by contrast, as he feels himself losing all definition and failing to 'hold this visible shape', sees the separate and removable pieces of his armour as symbolic of his own fragmenting identity: 'No more a soldier; bruised pieces go' (4.14.14, 43). Yet this same term is the one that Cleopatra chooses to restore the image of Antony to wholeness after his death. When Dolabella responds to her climactic speech of praise by denying that such a paragon of a man ever really existed, Cleopatra insists that her Antony was not fantasy but 'nature's piece 'gainst fancy, / Condemning shadows quite' (5.2.98–9).

Core scene: 4.4

This kind of rhetoric and staginess might be very hard to take if this was all there was to the play. But *Antony and Cleopatra* is much more volatile and varied than that. It keeps an audience engaged with Antony and Cleopatra at a very human level by allowing moments of humour, failure, warmth and intimacy to slip in between the cracks of the marmoreal rhetoric. A crucial scene in this respect is the one in which Antony puts on the very armour that he is later to take off with such self-awareness as part of the process of his own disintegration (above, 4.14.43). It is a scene of Shakespeare's invention, owing nothing to Plutarch. As the opening lines make clear, Antony has just risen from Cleopatra's bed (and this is as close to privacy as the play ever gets – the lovers are alone for just the first two lines, before Eros enters):

> MARK ANTONY
> Eros! Mine armour, Eros!
>
> CLEOPATRA
>   Sleep a little.
>
> MARK ANTONY
> No, my chuck. Eros! Come, mine armour, Eros!
>   (4.4.1–2)

Already the rhythm of these lines signals a brokenness which is as far as can be from the smooth and polished rhetoric of so much of their public interaction. Yet the competition and the struggle are still there, operating more honestly and affectionately than they do elsewhere in the play. The soldier and the lover compete for possession of Antony, and Cleopatra briefly tries to hold on to the lover before accepting the necessity of the soldier. As she begins to take on the new intimacy of arming him (usually a male-male intimacy), the unfamiliarity of the task allows their speech to continue in its more realistic broken rhythms and creates the space for wit and irony as well as affection:

CLEOPATRA
What's this for?

MARK ANTONY
   Ah, let be, let be! Thou art
The armourer of my heart. False, false! This, this!

CLEOPATRA
Sooth, la, I'll help. Thus it must be.

MARK ANTONY
      Well, well!
We shall thrive now.   (6–9)

An audience can scarcely fail to recall Cleopatra's betrayal of Antony in battle and her many occasions of falseness as they listen to this interchange. Yet its playfulness processes that pain in a healing way and shows the strength of the love that betrayed Antony's manhood.

Interestingly it is this scene, rather than a more male-oriented, military scene, into which Shakespeare scripts both Antony's awareness of his own prowess as a soldier (a 'workman in't' (18) he calls himself, meaning a truly skilled worker) and his love of the soldier's occupation: 'To business that we love we rise betime / And go to't with delight' (20–1). The first line is spoken to Cleopatra, the second to a soldier who comes to announce that Antony's men are waiting for him. Though the scene demonstrates the fullness of Antony's love for Cleopatra, it does not script any regret on leaving her. On the contrary, the shouting and flourish of trumpets offstage, the arrival of more soldiers and his warmth towards his men ('Tis well blown, lads' (25)) all highlight this departure as a positive moment for Antony. He truly becomes a soldier as he puts his armour on, and these lines are spoken as the arming is completed. His farewell is the farewell of a man who has consciously constructed himself (with the help of Cleopatra as well as Eros) as a 'man of steel' in this scene:

> Fare thee well, dame. Whate'er becomes of me,
> This is a soldier's kiss. [*Kisses her.*] Rebukable
> And worthy shameful check it were, to stand
> On more mechanic compliment. I'll leave thee
> Now like a man of steel.   (29–33)

Cleopatra's loss, left alone at the end of this scene, is tangible, and her lines break down almost completely:

> He goes forth gallantly. That he and Caesar might
> Determine this great war in single fight!
> Then Antony – but now –. Well, on. (36–8)

Real feeling rather than performance seems to be what this moment is about.

Performance

As such it is a rare moment for Cleopatra. She, even more than Antony, is not tormented by the gap between acting and being, as Hamlet is. For her acting *is* being. As a 'piece of work', she may seem momentarily achieved and complete, but the process of manufacturing that impression is one of artifice:

> since my lord
> Is Antony again, I will be Cleopatra.
> (3.13.190–1)

This highly 'performed' aspect of the play may be one reason why it has been so rarely filmed and so relatively unsuccessful when it has. Where on stage such conscious performance has a register ranging from tragic elevation to mere staginess, the medium of film tends towards making all high-register performance look undesirably stagy. And if the actress playing Cleopatra tries to play down the grandeur of the role, the critics will tend to say, as they did of Hildegard Neil and Janet Suzman in the film and video versions of 1972 and 1974, that they are simply not up to the requirements of the part.

This play takes the metatheatrical awareness which attaches transiently to the historic moment of Caesar's assassination in *Julius Caesar* (chapter 4 above) and disperses it across the whole play, allowing Antony and Cleopatra to play themselves as epic lovers throughout.[7] This performance, however, though pervasive, is not continuous. We have already examined one scene that breaks the mould with intimate ordinariness; but Shakespeare has other ways of showing the seams of this performance. One is to portray it as embarrassing childishness and quasi-rehearsal, as in Act 1, scene 3. Here Cleopatra picks a quarrel, challenges Antony to act his part and then criticises his acting.

CLEOPATRA
　　　　　Good now, play one scene
Of excellent dissembling, and let it look
Like perfect honour.

MARK ANTONY
　　　　　You'll heat my blood. No more.

CLEOPATRA
You can do better yet, but this is meetly [reasonably good].

MARK ANTONY
Now, by my sword –

CLEOPATRA
                And target. Still he mends,
But this is not the best. Look, prithee, Charmian,
How this Herculean Roman does become
The carriage of his chafe [grace the performance of his anger].
                        (1.3.79–86)

Another is to have a third party anticipate or comment on such behaviour, as Enobarbus does on hearing of Fulvia's death, which is the trigger for this quarrel:

> Cleopatra, catching but the least noise of this, dies instantly. I have seen her die twenty times upon far poorer moment. I do think there is mettle in death which commits some loving act upon her, she hath such a celerity in dying.   (1.2.147–51)

An even more daring and risky strategy of exposure is to script a botched performance, as in the case of Antony's suicide. Scripting Eros, Antony's follower, to perform his own suicide with perfect Stoic nobility makes Antony's performance look even poorer; and the undermining of Antony's struggle to look noble continues, first with the physical awkwardness and near-comedy of having Cleopatra and her women haul him up to the monument and then by having Antony repeat his best line, thus further reducing his tragic aspirations to mere pathos: 'I am dying, Egypt, dying' (4.15.19, 43). The risk of creating pathos, even absurdity, rather than tragedy is all the higher because Antony's death is not necessary. It is the consequence of Cleopatra taking performance a stage too far in seeking a way to avoid Antony's anger:

CLEOPATRA
                To th'monument!
Mardian, go tell him I have slain myself.
Say that the last I spoke was 'Antony',
And word it, prithee, piteously.
                        (4.13.6–9)

This play is unique, however, in giving the climactic death to a woman. If the play is to be seen as a tragedy, it will have to be Cleopatra's death, not Antony's, that ultimately determines that perspective. The risks that the last scene takes with tragic form are truly breathtaking. Shakespeare takes care to make the audience see the mixture of emotions and motivations that underpin Cleopatra's decision to die. She first gives voice to the sense that 'it is great /

To do that thing that ends all other deeds' (5.2.4–5), but immediately after that lofty utterance we see her again planning, measuring, weighing one course against another and acting the fraudulent part of Caesar's victim while she tries to outwit him. The near-song of her praise of Antony is framed on either side with pragmatic cunning, as she first pretends submission to Caesar, then pretends to have given him all her treasure. As if the shame and embarrassment of being discovered at this game were not enough, she is then depicted as fearful of an even worse shame in her eyes, the shame of being performed:

> The quick comedians
> Extemporally will stage us and present
> Our Alexandrian revels; Antony
> Shall be brought drunken forth; and I shall see
> Some squeaking Cleopatra boy my greatness
> I' the posture of a whore.   (5.2.215–20)

To script the boy-actor playing Cleopatra to voice this fear is to come as close to the edge of irony as it is possible to come, allowing the audience to sidestep their emotional engagement with the gathering tragic climax even as that progress continues.

As Cleopatra sends for her 'best attires', demanding that her women show her 'like a queen' (226–7), the echo of Antony turning himself into a soldier by dressing up as one, while also suggesting the gap between performer and role through the word 'like' (as in 'like a man of steel', above), is strong. We remember Antony's embarrassingly badly performed suicide and wait to see whether Cleopatra can perform a nobler death. Her ability to joke, even about playing a part, seems to face in two directions, continuing the clash of perspectives that is so characteristic of this play:

> Now, noble Charmian, we'll dispatch indeed,
> And when thou hast done this chare [chore], I'll give thee leave
> To play till doomsday.   (229–31)

It deflects the audience from empathy but it also removes the possibility of seeing Cleopatra as the object of irony, since she herself supplies the ironic take on this performance.

The flicking between high and low registers continues, at even shorter intervals. One moment Cleopatra is constructing herself as 'marble-constant' (239); the next she is engaging, as Hamlet does shortly before his death, in prose discourse with a clown. This Clown, as in *Hamlet*, has a direct link to death: where Hamlet's interlocutor digs Ophelia's grave, Cleopatra's brings 'the pretty worm of Nilus . . . / That kills and pains not' (242–3). Shakespeare reminds us here, as he does again in the closing speech of the play, that Cleopatra has 'pursued conclusions infinite / Of easy ways to die' (354–5). If she achieves tragic grandeur, it will be in the teeth of comic and bathetic opposition. Indeed she can barely get the clown off stage in order to pursue her death.

But when she does, it is with calm authority and easy elevation that she begins to set her death in motion:

> Give me my robe. Put on my crown. I have
> Immortal longings in me.   (279–80)

The echo of, and competition with, Antony, is still audible; and yet somehow the competition begins to seem more like completion. If Cleopatra can pull off tragic dignity, it seems, that will redeem and give value to Antony's death. As she holds the serpent to her breast she does indeed seem to become finally 'marble-constant'. Like Hamlet holding Yorick's skull, she becomes a meaningful, though more conflicted, emblem, pointing towards concupiscence as well as mortality. Caesar's praise too seems to endorse the tragic seriousness her death aspires to. Though he knows and says that she investigated easy ways to die, he still calls her 'Bravest at the last' and 'royal' in her decision to take her own life (334–5). The move backwards out of the story, the metanarrative moment of Caesar's last speech, restores to both Antony and Cleopatra the epic status they have so often compromised:

> No grave upon the earth shall clip in it
> A pair so famous. High events as these
> Strike those that make them, and their story is
> No less in pity than his glory which
> Brought them to be lamented.   (358–62)

In awarding himself glory, Caesar asks for both pity and recognition of greatness for the lovers. He, at least, invites the audience to see their end as tragic.

Chapter 11

Coriolanus

Following the scripting of a central female figure and a playful opening up and crossing of genders in *Antony and Cleopatra*, this play returns to the male-dominated world of *Julius Caesar* and *Timon of Athens*. Like all three of those earlier plays, its source is North's Plutarch, and like *Antony*, *Julius Caesar* and *Titus Andronicus*, it is set in Rome; but where *Antony* and *Julius Caesar* were set in the last days of the Roman Republic, *Coriolanus* is set much earlier, soon after its establishment following the expulsion of the Tarquins. The exploration of what it means to be Roman reaches a new intensity in this play; but at the same time its links with contemporary Jacobean politics are more directly topical than those of any of Shakespeare's earlier tragedies. Where *Julius Caesar*, for example, may point to the general political unease of the late 1590s and to questions of government made sharper by the looming problem of a successor to Elizabeth, *Coriolanus* points very specifically to the Midlands Rising of 1607 and possibly also to clashes between James and his parliaments and to the process of parliamentary selection, matters widely discussed, according to Robert Cecil, Secretary of State: 'Parliamentary matters are ordinarily talked of in the streets. I have heard myself, being in my coach, these words spoken aloud: "God prosper those that further the overthrow of these monopolies. God send the prerogative touch not our liberty."'[1] Though Cecil was writing in 1601, matters of liberty and prerogative (sovereign right) remained of central concern throughout the reign of James I and are also central to this play. *Timon*, *Lear* and *Macbeth* allude quite closely to matters of court and state, but *Coriolanus* is unusual in engaging so directly with a popular event like a rising, and one that bore more closely on Shakespeare's Stratford connections than on his connections with the court via the King's Men; for the Midlands Rising, as the name indicates, took place across several Midlands counties, including Warwickshire.

The people

Like *Julius Caesar*, the play opens with a group of citizens; these ones, however, are not celebrating, but rioting. The opening stage direction, which may be

140

Shakespeare's, describes them as '*mutinous*' and has them entering '*with staves, clubs, and other weapons*'.[2] And hunger is immediately identified as the cause of their rebellion: 'You are all resolved rather to die than to famish?' (1.1.3–4). One of the ways in which the play signals its topicality is by its alteration to the source: where in Plutarch the people riot against unregulated usury, in Shakespeare they riot because of food shortages.[3] The Midlands Rising was directed in the first instance against enclosures, but food shortage emerged as a secondary complaint in its wake, and by June 1608 James had issued two proclamations seeking to control the use of grain.[4] Shakespeare was also more personally familiar with food shortage and hoarding: he was named in 1598 for having illegally hoarded ten quarters (eighty bushels) of malt or corn during one such shortage.[5]

This play differs notably from *Julius Caesar* in presenting the people as neither comic nor of one mind. They are not simply a mob, but have different views and reasonable cause for distress. In their attitudes towards Caius Martius (later Coriolanus), moreover, we see some attempt to be fair-minded. Thus the First Citizen sees clearly the problem of need versus excess (a problem which Lear finally comes to understand), and his vocabulary is similar to Lear's, though spoken from a much lower place in the social hierarchy:

> What authority surfeits on would relieve us. If they would yield us but
> the superfluity while it were wholesome, we might guess they relieved us
> humanely; but they think we are too dear: the leanness that afflicts us,
> the object of our misery, is as an inventory to particularise their
> abundance; our sufferance is a gain to them. Let us revenge this with our
> pikes, ere we become rakes. For the gods know, I speak this in hunger for
> bread, not in thirst for revenge.   (1.1.15–24)

Attitudes to Martius are as divided as they are about Antony in the opening scene of *Antony and Cleopatra*, comprising both the clear-sighted, if somewhat hostile, view of the First Citizen and the plea for sympathy of the Second Citizen:

> FIRST CITIZEN
> though soft-conscienced men can be content to say it was for his country,
> he did it to please his mother, and to be partly proud, which he is, even
> to the altitude of his virtue.
>
> SECOND CITIZEN
> What he cannot help in his nature, you account a vice in him.
>
> (1.1.36–41)

Brecht, who saw in Shakespeare this capacity for showing both sides of an issue, adapted the play for performance, and published a discussion of the first scene.

It is evident that this play interested him because, as one of his actors puts it, 'it is written realistically, and includes sufficient material of a contradictory sort'.[6] For Brecht, it was above all a tragedy of the Roman people, not of the central protagonist.

Menenius Agrippa seeks to calm the citizens with a metaphor that posits the people as mutinous limbs against the senate as the belly of the state, seemingly inactive and self-satisfying, but in fact nurturing (a piece of rhetoric that blatantly substitutes for a practical response to the people's demand for food); but the metaphor barely masks his polarised view of the clash between patrician and plebeian. 'Rome and her rats are at the point of battle', he concludes; 'the one side must have bale [pain, misfortune]' (1.1.161–2). Shakespeare uses this moment of clarity to cue Martius' entry, with his undisguised contempt for the common people:

> What's the matter, you dissentious rogues
> That, rubbing the poor itch of your opinion,
> Make yourselves scabs?   (1.1.163–5)

and throughout the play Martius refers to the people in abusive terms. His response to their need is open aggression:

> Would the nobility lay aside their ruth,
> And let me use my sword, I'd make a quarry
> With thousands of these quarter'd slaves, as high
> As I could pick my lance.   (1.1.196–9)

In reporting the creation of the tribunes in response to another group of rebellious citizens elsewhere in the city, Martius can scarcely be bothered to name them as individuals:

> Five tribunes to defend their vulgar wisdoms,
> Of their own choice. One's Junius Brutus,
> Sicinius Velutus, and I know not.
>   (1.1.214–16)

The moment reverberates with another, later moment, when Martius himself is given the name, Coriolanus, that commemorates his heroic deeds at Corioles, while at the same he cannot remember the name of the man whose liberty he wants to redeem for his kindness to him:

> CORIOLANUS
> I sometime lay here in Corioles,
> At a poor man's house: he us'd me kindly.
> He cried to me. I saw him prisoner.

But then Aufidius was within my view,
And wrath o'erwhelm'd my pity. I request you
To give my poor host freedom.

COMINIUS

                          Oh well begg'd!
Were he the butcher of my son, he should
Be free as is the wind. Deliver him, Titus.

LARTIUS

Martius, his name?

CORIOLANUS

                          By Jupiter, forgot!
I am weary, yea, my memory is tired;
Have we no wine here?   (1.9.80–90)

This is a moment deliberately altered from the source. In Plutarch the man is unnamed, though known to Coriolanus, and the act remains a mark of Coriolanus' magnanimity; but in Shakespeare the potential for magnanimity is undercut by his careless forgetting of the name and his swift dismissal of that failure as trivial. A certain attitude towards ordinary people is scripted here as clearly as through explicit aggression.

The thing itself

As one of the tribunes comments, in response to Coriolanus' expressed aversion to 'the mutable, rank-scented meinie [multitude]':

                 You speak o' th' people,
       As if you were a god to punish, not
       A man of their infirmity.

                 (3.1.65, 79–81)

The tribunes are represented as unworthy, even despicable, themselves, yet they are given occasionally powerful lines in defence of the people. Sicinius surely has a point that echoes through the play when he asks rhetorically 'What is the city but the people?' (3.1.197). Coriolanus, however, is represented as notably separate from the community throughout, by way of both his military superiority and his contempt for almost all other men: 'he is himself alone, / To answer all the city' (1.4.51–2);[7] 'O me alone! Make you a sword of me!' (1.6.76);[8] 'Alone I fought' (1.8.8); 'all alone Martius did fight' (2.1.161); 'alone he enter'd' (2.2.110); 'I banish you!' (3.3.123); 'I go alone, / Like to a lonely dragon'

(4.1.29–30); 'Alone I did it' (5.6.116). Coriolanus was John Philip Kemble's most famous part, and one with which his biographer, James Boaden, saw him identifying especially closely when, as manager of Covent Garden Theatre, he confronted audiences rioting against rises in ticket prices.[9] Olivier's performance for a later age created the 'bizarre impression of one man lynching a crowd'.[10]

In writing *Coriolanus* Shakespeare may have had in mind, as perhaps also in *Timon*, the well-known Aristotelian dictum that a solitary man was either a beast or a god. Certainly Coriolanus is repeatedly described in non-human terms, and the word 'thing' is recurrent. It is as though, having experimented in Antony with a Roman who is all too human despite his astounding capacity for endurance, Shakespeare now explores a Roman masculinity that excludes such human weakness:

> COMINIUS
> He was a thing of blood;
>
> > (2.2.109)
>
> AUFIDIUS
> Thou noble thing;
>
> > (4.5.117)
>
> COMINIUS
> He is their god. He leads them like a thing
> Made by some other deity than nature,
> That shapes man better;   (4.6.91–3)
>
> AUFIDIUS
> Not to be other than one thing, not moving
> From th'casque to th'cushion;   (4.7.42–3)
>
> MENENIUS
> This Martius is grown from man to dragon: he has wings: he's more than a creeping thing . . . When he walks, he moves like an engine and the ground shrinks before his treading.   (5.4.12–20)

Coriolanus can also be even less than a thing, as Cominius implies: 'He was a kind of nothing, titleless, / Till he had forg'd himself a name o' th'fire / Of burning Rome' (5.1.13–15). He becomes a thing, something, in battle; his *virtus* is undeniable, if inhuman. But outside battle he is considerably less than that.

The words 'thing' and 'nothing' also reverberate, of course, in *King Lear*, but very differently. Where Lear's recognition of '[u]naccommodated man' as 'the thing itself' (3.4.95) is a discovery of what is valuable about humanity, the descriptions of Coriolanus as a thing represent the distance between his way of being and that of common humanity. The 'thing' that he is is not a bedrock of value but the absence of it. When he voices his determination not to acknowledge his ties to family the very terms of his expression confirm the unnaturalness of such a resolution:

> I'll never
> Be such a gosling to obey instinct, but stand
> As if a man were author of himself
> And knew no other kin.   (5.3.34–7)

Lear, damaged in a way that Coriolanus is not, by unloving and unnatural daughters, learns common humanity in that abyss; even Timon, apparently without family ties, is unable to shake off his faithful steward.

In the end, however, Coriolanus too, despite aspiring to a condition of pure independence, is forced to recognise the ties that bind him. The approach of his mother, wife and son to persuade him not to destroy Rome, which is what provokes his statement of intention not to obey instinct, forces him into an acceptance of the impossibility of being fully alone and yet fully human. As in *Lear*, the kneeling of parent to child drives home the untenable reversal of duty and authority. When Volumnia kneels to her son, accompanied by Valeria, Virgilia and Coriolanus' son, Coriolanus is reduced to silence, as the unusually eloquent stage direction highlights: '*Holds her by the hand silent*' (5.3.183). And Coriolanus himself voices the link between that yielding and his death, which must inevitably follow at the hands of the now betrayed Volsces (5.3.185–9).

Manhood and family

As the silent intensity of this held tableau suggests, the hero's relationship with his mother is given unusual prominence in this play, and Shakespeare gives this relationship a much stronger presence than it has in Plutarch. Paradoxically in the male-dominated world of this play, three women have a role to play, and two of them, wife and mother to Coriolanus, represent respectively the extremes of passive and dominant womanhood. Comparison with Brutus' wife, Portia, is revealing. As discussed in chapter 4 above, Portia is simultaneously an obedient, virtuous and assertive wife. She justifies her right to share her husband's worries and implicitly challenges his Stoic withholding of emotional expression by wounding her own thigh, thereby demonstrating that it is possible to combine emotional affect with Stoic endurance. These contradictory aspects of female being are in *Coriolanus* divided between the silent and submissive Virgilia, whose dominant feeling about her husband is fear for his safety, and the fierce, even warlike, Volumnia, whose regard for the Roman male concept of *virtus* is so high that she revels in the wounds her son acquires in battle, insisting to Virgilia that

> The breasts of Hecuba
> When she did suckle Hector, look'd not lovelier
> Than Hector's forehead when it spit forth blood.
>
> (1.3.40–2)

Thus, while one woman seeks to temper Coriolanus' fiercely Roman masculinity, the other nourishes it, seeing a parallel between mother's milk and male blood spilt in battle. Providing and withholding nourishment are in fact tied up throughout the play with warfare, wounding and masculinity, as critics such as Adelman, Cavell and Kahn have shown.[11]

The fact that the play opens with demands for food and offers up Menenius' extended fable of the belly as a response to those demands presents an image which is central to the nexus of meanings the play makes and one which has the potential to produce strong psychological as well as political readings. As Stanley Cavell comments, '[b]oth perspectives are . . . interested in who produces food and in how food is distributed and paid for'.[12] Janet Adelman links the play's food riots with the image of the mother who does not feed her child enough, observing that one scarcely needs a psychoanalytic approach 'to notice that Volumnia is not a nourishing mother' and citing as representative of Volumnia's withholding attitude her rejection of Menenius' invitation to dinner following Coriolanus' banishment: 'Anger's my meat: I sup upon myself / And so shall starve with feeding' (4.2.50–1).[13] Her vision of blood shed in battle as parallel with mother's milk suggests something of the kind of masculinity she has nurtured in her son; and his dependency on her in turn suggests the continuing, unsatisfied hunger such bitter nourishment fosters. The strong 'I am' of Coriolanus, while it recalls the assertiveness of earlier Shakespearean tragic heroes, has a hollow ring in this play, where the protagonist's determination to renounce kin, friendship and country is presented as both sterile and impossible.

Coriolanus, as Cavell notes, characteristically withholds from his fellow-Romans: both food and good words. When he speaks he speaks to reject communication. In a similar way, he tries to withold himself even as he unwillingly shows his wounds. The only kind of reciprocity he finds easy is reciprocal aggression. When Rome is attacked, he attacks her attackers; when Rome banishes him, he banishes Rome and turns his attack against it. Where in *Timon of Athens* the hero merely withdraws from his city and from the ties that bind him to humanity, and so dies, in *Coriolanus* the hero mounts an attack on his city (as Alcibiades does in *Timon*); but where Alcibiades' mercy is portrayed as an act of strength, Coriolanus' mercy is unwillingly given, elicited only by the pleading of women. (In *Macbeth*, by contrast, women have to be eliminated from the play for Macbeth to be able to maintain an inhuman level of brutality to the end.) Both Timon and Coriolanus are presented as ultimately self-consuming; their attempts to withdraw from the relationships that bind them into humanity result in their own destruction. A man, both must learn, cannot deny his relationship and kinship with family or friends.

Core scene: 4.4

Coriolanus' appearance before the city of Antium '*in mean apparel, disguised and muffled*' represents the climax of a relationship explored from the beginning of the play, between himself and the only warrior to match him, the Volscian leader Tullus Aufidius. In Plutarch, Aufidius is not mentioned before this point in the narrative; but in Shakespeare's play a rivalry and consequent bond between the two men is built up from Act 1 on.[14] The first mention of him in the play is Martius' admission of envious admiration for him:

> I sin in envying his nobility;
> And were I anything but what I am,
> I would wish me only he;
>
> (1.1.229–31)

and it is the sight of Aufidius that later causes wrath to overwhelm Coriolanus' pity and forget the name of his host (pp. 142–3 above). He wants to know if Aufidius speaks of him, wants to hear what he has said and longs for an excuse to seek him out at Antium 'To oppose his hatred fully' (3.1.20). Aufidius himself first appears at 1.2, where he makes clear that his rivalry with Martius is understood by both of them as one that must be pursued to the death:

> If we and Caius Martius chance to meet,
> 'Tis sworn between us, we shall ever strike
> Till one can do no more.   (1.2.34–6)

When Martius appears outside Antium in 4.4, he is between two cities, exiled from Rome, existing in a space barely imaginable for a warrior, outside any community he may be called upon to defend. As discussed in chapter 7 above, location outside city walls (and the stage doors, by convention, make the presence of a city wall visible throughout this scene) can offer a powerfully iconic representation of social exclusion, even exclusion from full humanity. It is in this interstitial space that Coriolanus, only briefly alone despite his ever-present desire for singularity, speaks his only private soliloquy of the play. It is a soliloquy in two halves, both apostrophes, the first to the city of Antium, the second to the world in general. Addressing Antium first, his tone his difficult to assess:

> A goodly city is this Antium. City,
> 'Tis I that made thy widows: many an heir
> Of these fair edifices 'fore my wars
> Have I heard groan, and drop. Then know me not;
> Lest that thy wives with spits, and boys with stones,
> In puny battle slay me.   (4.4.1–6)

Is this mere boasting, such as we have heard before? Or is there any remorse, or even fear, now that he is alone with only his disguise to protect him from the revenge of the Volsces? In Plutarch his arrival at Antium follows several days of inner turmoil as Coriolanus wonders how to proceed; and 'in the end', writes Plutarch, he could settle on 'no way to take a profitable or honourable course, but only was pricked forward still to be revenged of the Romans'.[15] The aim of revenge, constructed by Plutarch in opposition to honour, does not emerge in Shakespeare's play until the next scene, so that the question of Coriolanus' motives in coming to Antium is left more open at this point. His soliloquies are thus of real interest to an audience being offered the opportunity to see Coriolanus' mind at work privately for the first and only time.

Interrupting the soliloquy that shapes this brief scene is another unique moment: Coriolanus speaking courteously to a citizen. He asks for directions to Aufidius' house, with a polite greeting, further polite forms ('if it be your will', 'beseech you' (7, 10)) and final thanks and farewell. Elsewhere in the play his characteristic mode of interaction with common citizens is contemptuous and dismissive, if not abusive. Again we are led to wonder why Shakespeare adds this brief exchange to his source. Is it evidence that Coriolanus can be as civil as any other man when not riled by the demands of Roman forms of government, or is it another possible indicator of fear in a place where he knows his life is at risk if he steps out of line? Either way, it opens up sides of the man hitherto unseen in the play.

The second half of the soliloquy meditates on the sudden 'slippery turns' of the world, imagining close friends turning to enmity and enemies becoming friends through 'some trick not worth an egg' (21), as he stands between the place he once loved, but now hates, and the place he once fought against, but now plans to enter. The speech becomes more personally intense and invested as it closes with allusive reference to an unnamed 'he':

> if he slay me
> He does fair justice; if he give me way,
> I'll do his country service.   (23–5)

'He' is of course Aufidius, and this conspicuous withholding of his name is one of the ways in which the scene signals his central importance. The soliloquy's extended consideration of love between

> Friends now fast sworn,
> Whose double bosoms seems to wear one heart,
> Whose hours, whose bed, whose meal and exercise
> Are still together, who twin, as 'twere, in love
> Unseparable   (11–16)

begins to make sense within the context of Coriolanus' driving urge to meet the one man he feels to be truly worthy of his love, because he represents the acme of the warrior. Aufidius fulfils the Roman ideal of *virtus* in a way that transcends nationhood. If Coriolanus has any fear in the earlier part of the scene, it is perhaps a fear of dying before the consummation of this meeting is achieved. To be slain by a random citizen or a mob of anonymous Volsces would deny him the right to come face to face with the worthy opponent he has so long singled out in battle.

Aufidius' reception of Coriolanus in the following scene confirms the intensity of longing for this meeting as mutual:

> Let me twine
> Mine arms about that body,
> . . .
> Know thou first,
> I lov'd the maid I married; never man
> Sigh'd truer breath; but that I see thee here,
> Thou noble thing, more dances my rapt heart
> Than when I first my wedded mistress saw
> Bestride my threshold.   (4.5.107–8, 114–19)

And this is a mere extract from a thirty-four-line speech by Aufidius. Clearly Coriolanus is bound by ties beyond and in addition to those of kin. The homosocial bond that creates such desire between two men who share both an understanding of what constitutes heroic masculinity, and an outstanding capacity for performing it, is as crucial to Coriolanus' identity and to the meaning of the play as the bond with his mother, which, with its nourishing of *virtus*, helped to create it.

Performance

There is, then, only one kind of performance that seems natural to Coriolanus, namely that of *virtus*. The importance of this necessarily stands out in a play where so much time is given over to exploring what it feels like to be forced into a performance that feels alien to identity. And both these ways of constructing the relationship between performance and identity are markedly different from the approach of *Antony and Cleopatra*, which investigates the shaping of identity by an overwhelming urge *to* perform. Though discussion of both these plays ends with a section on 'Performance', the subject is one that marks the distance between them. Coriolanus, unlike Antony or Cleopatra, loathes the very idea of conscious performance; but the inherent tension between his natural characteristics and his need to win the voices of the people if he wishes to become consul requires that he perform. As Plutarch describes his nature, 'he was so choleric and impatient, that he would yield to no living creature: which made him churlish, uncivil, and altogether unfit for any man's conversation . . . [other men] could not be acquainted with him, as one citizen useth to be with another in the city. His behaviour was so unpleasant to them, by reason of a certain insolent and stern manner he had, which because it was too lordly, was disliked.'[16]

Coriolanus was also, Plutarch notes within the same passage, marvellously constant, 'never overcome with pleasure, nor money', capable of enduring 'all manner of pains and travails' and admired for 'his stoutness and temperancy'; but none of these qualities is enough to overcome his rooted incivility. Every attempt on the part of those close to him to make him temper that incivility is regarded by Coriolanus as an imposition of falseness. Having been persuaded by Menenius and Volumnia to show the people his wounds and ask for their voices, only to find himself unable to maintain the required level of civility, he asks his mother:

> Why did you wish me milder? Would you have me
> False to my nature? Rather say I play
> The man I am.   (3.2.14–16)

As they seek to persuade him to return and try again, Volumnia and Cominius openly adopt the vocabulary of performance and instruct him as a director might instruct an actor:

VOLUMNIA
        I prithee now, my son,
Go to them, with this bonnet in thy hand,
And thus far having stretch'd it – here be with them –
Thy knee bussing the stones – for in such business
Action is eloquence . . .   (3.2.72–6)

CORIOLANUS
You have put me now to such a part which never
I shall discharge to th'life.

COMINIUS
               Come, come, we'll prompt you.
                      (3.2.105–7)

In agreeing to play the part, Coriolanus takes as metaphor the lowest kind of performer, a mountebank (an itinerant charlatan): 'Chide me no more. I'll mountebank their loves' (3.2.132). He cannot of course hold the line, and his next attempt to woo the people collapses almost immediately, resulting in his banishment by popular consent. As soon as he leaves the company of Roman citizens and the need to put himself on display, the vocabulary of performance disappears. It is notably absent from the scene discussed as core above, even though he is there in disguise and more literally like an actor. It recurs, however, at the point where he is beginning to be overcome, against his will, by the need to yield to his family's plea to spare Rome:

        Like a dull actor now
I have forgot my part, and I am out,
Even to a full disgrace.   (5.3.40–2)

Finding himself genuinely moved by their pleading, he cannot maintain his determination to banish instinct and affection and cannot perform the Roman masculinity which is the only kind of being he has hitherto accommodated within his own sense of identity. Even though he is driven to this new way of being by spontaneous feeling, he experiences it as an alien role because it is so unfamiliar.

    It is inevitable, as Coriolanus himself knows, that this yielding to emotion will lead to his death. In setting mercy and honour at difference within himself, as Aufidius puts it (5.3.200–1), he simultaneously breaks the terms of his agreement with the Volsces and destroys the possibility of a unified identity for himself. In becoming more than a thing by acknowledging bonds of love and pity, he loses the impregnability as well as the hollowness of being a thing. Aufidius is able to represent Coriolanus' peace with Rome as a shameful, 'whin[ing]' response to 'his nurse's tears'; and where the name of 'Coriolanus' once defined its bearer by his martial skill and resolution, this act of humanity now redefines him, in Aufidius' eyes, as a 'boy of tears' (5.6.97, 101). Without this acknowledgement of humanity, however, it is doubtful whether the play could be a tragedy. *Timon of Athens*, it was argued in chapter 7, cannot be fully tragic because the hero persists in an absolute rejection of humanity to the end. His offstage reported death and several epitaphs leave Alcibiades' closing affirmation of his nobility sounding curiously pointless, almost token. Coriolanus' onstage death, by contrast, follows the more recognisable pattern of earlier Shakespearean tragic deaths. He dies demonstrating heroic defiance as he again stands alone against enemies who outnumber him, a posture familiar throughout the play, but now inflected by the acknowledgement of human ties that has exposed him to his enemies in this way. Order and dignity are restored as his enemies praise his greatness and take up the body for ceremonial exit, and the formal martial close is reminiscent of *Hamlet*. As in *Hamlet*, where it is important that Horatio should survive to tell Hamlet's story so that his reputation is not tarnished, the closing emphasis is on the nobility of the trace the tragic hero leaves behind: 'Yet he shall have a noble memory' (5.6.153). It is an emphasis made the more powerful by the fact that it is spoken by the man who is at once Coriolanus' killer, his greatest rival and perhaps the human being with whom he has felt the closest affinity.

Notes

Introduction

1 The term is central to Williams' work, highlighting the way in which ways of being are culturally determined.
2 http://www.rsc.org.uk/lear/tragedy/bates.html [*sic*].
3 Emily Wilson, *Mocked with Death: Tragic Overliving from Sophocles to Milton* (Baltimore and London: Johns Hopkins University Press, 2004), 18–19.
4 The First Folio is the first collected volume of Shakespeare's plays, published in 1623, seven years after his death. A folio is a large and expensive volume. Those plays of Shakespeare's published during his lifetime (and only about half of them were) were produced individually in quarto, a smaller and much cheaper form of publication.
5 The fullest recent account of scholarship on this subject is Brian Vickers' *Shakespeare, Co-Author* (Oxford: Oxford University Press, 2002).

1 Tragedy before Shakespeare

1 *Preface to Shakespeare* (1765), in H. R. Woudhuysen, ed., *Samuel Johnson on Shakespeare* (London: Penguin, 1989), 127.
2 The Greek term τραγῳδία literally means 'goat-song', and different theories have been proposed for the association with goats.
3 On medieval awareness of tragedy and tragic theory, see further Timothy Reiss, 'Renaissance Theatre and the Theory of Tragedy', in *The Cambridge History of Literary Criticism, Volume 3, The Renaissance*, ed. Glyn P. Norton (Cambridge: Cambridge University Press, 1999), 232–4.
4 Bruce Smith, *Ancient Scripts and Modern Experience on the English Stage, 1500–1700* (Princeton: Princeton University Press, 1988), 204–5.
5 Elizabethan translators of Seneca, however, tended to exaggerate the rhetorical qualities of their original (see H. B. Charlton, *The Senecan Tradition in Renaissance Tragedy: A Re-issue of an Essay published in 1921* (Manchester: Manchester University Press, 1946), clvii–clviii). Robert Miola has discussed changing critical assessments of the extent of Seneca's influence in chapter 1 of his *Shakespeare and Classical Tragedy: The Influence of Seneca* (Oxford: Clarendon Press, 1992).

6 Smith, *Ancient Scripts*, 200–1. Seneca, however, was not the only influence on the development of five-act structure, though he was probably the main one in sixteenth-century England. Horace had advocated it; commentaries on Terence made reference to it; and it was also mediated through the Italian plays of Cinthio, himself strongly influenced by Seneca (Smith, *Ancient Scripts*, 204–5).

7 The possibility that Shakespeare knew Latin versions of some Greek tragedies cannot be completely ruled out. See Emrys Jones, *The Origins of Shakespeare* (Oxford: Clarendon Press, 1977), 85–118 and Louise Schleiner, 'Latinized Greek Drama in Shakespeare's Writing of *Hamlet*', *Shakespeare Quarterly* 41 (1990), 29–48.

8 These three definitions and more were brought together by Jonathan Bate in a lecture given to the Royal Shakespeare Company in 2004 and reproduced on the RSC website for the 2004–5 season of tragedies, http://www.rsc.org.uk/lear/tragedy/definitions.html.

9 Quotations from Aristotle's *Poetics* are taken from S. H. Butcher's translation, *Aristotle's Theory of Poetry and Fine Art, with a Critical Text and Translation of The Poetics*, 4th edn (New York: Dover Publications, 1951).

10 John Kerrigan, *Revenge Tragedy: Aeschylus to Armageddon* (Oxford: Clarendon Press, 1996), 111.

11 The probability of Shakespeare's reading of Sidney is demonstrated by a passage in *As You Like It* that seems to parody it. See Janette Dillon, *The Cambridge Introduction to Early English Theatre* (Cambridge: Cambridge University Press, 2006), 156.

12 Brian Vickers, ed., *English Renaissance Literary Criticism* (Oxford: Clarendon Press, 1999), 312.

13 It was in fact Castelvetro, whose commentary on Aristotle's *Poetics* was published in 1570, who insisted on the three unities of time, place and action. Italian European Renaissance commentators did discuss the concept of *catharsis* (see Reiss, 'Renaissance Theatre', 240–2), but this had very little effect on English theorists.

14 Prologue, line 37, in *The Works of Richard Edwards: Politics, Poetry and Performance in Sixteenth-Century England*, ed. Ros King (Manchester and New York: Manchester University Press, 2001). I discuss *King Cambyses* and *Damon and Pythias* more fully in chapter 4 of *Early English Theatre*, where questions of genre are also more broadly examined.

15 G. K. Hunter, 'Elizabethan Theatrical Genres and Literary Theory', in *The Cambridge History of Literary Criticism, Volume 3* (Cambridge: Cambridge University Press, 1999), 248.

16 He also wrote rather disapprovingly in the same preface of Shakespeare's characteristically mixed dramaturgy: 'In tragedy he is always struggling after some occasion to be comic' (Woudhuysen, ed., *Samuel Johnson on Shakespeare*, 128).

17 Quotations from *The Spanish Tragedy* are taken from J. R. Mulryne's edition (London and Tonbridge: Ernest Benn, 1970).

18 On the emblematic use of props see further Dillon, *Early English Theatre*, ch. 2.

19 Henslowe, the owner of the Rose, kept a note of the daily takings at the theatre. His so-called 'Diary', compiled over the period 1592–1603, is actually a mixture of different kinds of records, and remains our best guide to the day-to-day workings of an Elizabethan playhouse.

20 *Hubris* (meaning pride or presumption) is Aristotle's term.

21 The detail of their titles is of interest here, in the context of examining and defining what tragedy is (dates are of the earliest published editions): 'Tamburlaine the great. Who, from a Scythian shepherd, by his rare and wonderful conquests, became a most puissant and mighty monarch. And (for his tyranny, and terror in war) was termed, the scourge of God. Divided into two tragical discourses' (1590); 'The tragedy of Dido queen of Carthage' (1594); 'The troublesome reign and lamentable death of Edward the second, King of England, with the tragical fall of proud Mortimer: and also the life and death of Piers Gaveston, the great Earl of Cornwall, and mighty favourite of King Edward the Second' (1593); 'The tragical history of D. Faustus' (1604); 'The famous tragedy of the rich Jew of Malta' (1633).

22 Terry Eagleton lists some of the answers that have historically been offered to the question of why tragedy gives pleasure (*Sweet Violence: The Idea of the Tragic* (Malden, Mass. and Oxford: Blackwell, 2003), 168–77), and A. D. Nuttall has written a book-length study on the subject, *Why Does Tragedy Give Pleasure?* (Oxford: Clarendon Press, 1996).

23 Eagleton cites examples of plays from Greek tragedy onwards that cannot be said to have a tragic hero, and notes that Aristotle makes no mention of such a figure. His focus is on tragedy as action rather than character (*Sweet Violence*, 77; cf. Aristotle as cited on p. 12 above).

2 *Titus Andronicus*

1 For a summary and analysis of critical views on the authorship question, see Vickers, *Shakespeare, Co-Author*, ch. 3.

2 The Quarto text of *Othello* has incomplete act divisions, but it was printed in 1622, six years after Shakespeare's death and only a year before the Folio. Shakespeare must have known about five-act division. The choruses of *Henry V*, for example, indicate that he conceived of it in five parts, but the Quarto text has no act divisions and the Folio act divisions do not correspond to the placing of the choruses (which may be an editorial or printing error). *Romeo and Juliet* has two choruses, but none of the early printed texts, including the Folio, is divided into acts. See further Gary Taylor, 'The Structure of Performance: Act-intervals in the London Theatres, 1576–1642', in Gary Taylor and John Jowett, *Shakespeare Reshaped 1606–23* (Oxford: Clarendon Press, 1993), 3–50; Wilfred T. Jewkes, *Act Division in Elizabethan and Jacobean Plays, 1583–1616* (New York: AMS Press, 1972); and Emrys Jones, *Scenic*

Form in Shakespeare (Oxford: Clarendon Press, 1971). I will, however, sometimes use the terminology of acts and scenes in this and subsequent chapters for ease of reference to modern texts that routinely retain that division.

3 Some Elizabethan playhouses had only two openings in the tiring house wall (as illustrated in the famous De Witt sketch), while others had three. Stage directions from other plays at the Rose indicate that it must have had a central opening in addition to the two doors, but the terminology here of 'one door' and 'the other' probably indicates that the central opening had no door, but may have been curtained at times. See Scott McMillin, 'The Rose and the Swan', in *The Development of Shakespeare's Theatre*, ed. John H. Astington, AMS Studies in the Renaissance, 24 (New York: AMS, 1992), 159–83. On the design and features of Elizabethan playhouses more generally, see further Andrew Gurr, *The Shakespearean Stage, 1574–1642*, 3rd edn (Cambridge: Cambridge University Press, 1992) and Andrew Gurr and M. Ichikawa, *Staging in Shakespeare's Theatres* (Oxford: Oxford University Press, 2000).

4 Jonathan Bate discusses the practical problems of a chariot entry in his note to line 253 of the Arden edition (London: Routledge, 1995).

5 For further discussion of the drawing and its implications, see Bate, Introduction, 41–3; R. A. Foakes, *Illustrations of the English Stage, 1580–1642* (Stanford, California: Stanford University Press, 1985), 48–51; and June Schlueter, "Rereading the Peacham Drawing', *Shakespeare Quarterly* 50 (1999), 171–84. Schlueter argues that the drawing depicts a sequence from a different play about Titus Andronicus performed by English actors in Germany.

6 See Gustav Ungerer, 'An Unrecorded Elizabethan Performance of *Titus Andronicus*', *Shakespeare Survey* 14 (1961), 102–9.

7 The Athenian view of blood-sacrifice as religious purification is made explicit for example, in Sophocles' *Oedipus Rex*, when Oedipus asks: 'What purification is required?' and Creon replies 'The banishment of a man, or the payment of blood for blood / For the shedding of blood is the cause of our city's peril' (lines 98–100, in *The Theban Plays: Oedipus the King, Oedipus at Colonus, Antigone*, trans. E. F. Watling (Harmondsworth: Penguin, 1947)).

8 The quotation is from Jasper Heywood's translation of *Thyestes*, in the *Chadwyck-Healy Database of English Drama*, http://lion.chadwyck.co.uk.

9 In a sense this move from ritual to revenge parallels the progress of tragedy itself, initially conceived as part of a religious rite in Athens, but losing that context in its Senecan reworking. The acts of violence performed on stage in *Titus* would have been proscribed in Greek tragedy as a violation of the sanctity of ritual. See further Charlton, *Senecan Tradition*, xix–xxiii, who describes how 'the theme of personal Revenge' in Senecan tragedy supersedes that of 'divine Retribution' in Greek tragedy (xxii).

10 Again, Bate discusses the practical problems of a real chariot in his note to this line.

11 Muriel Bradbrook draws attention to the presence of the dumb-show of 'the bloody banquet', involving a table set with black candles and skulls as drinking vessels, in

non-Shakespearean plays (*Themes and Conventions of Elizabethan Tragedy*, 2nd edn (Cambridge: Cambridge University Press, 1980), 19).

12 Some editors emend 'father and mother' to 'father, brother', on grounds that seem to me insufficient. See Bate, Introduction, 120–1 for further discussion.

13 Bate, Introduction, 121.

14 Some have argued that *Julius Caesar* is a revenge play, but it is clearly very far from the Senecan prototype of a revenge play.

15 On Roman history and Shakespeare's handling of it see further Bate, Introduction, 16–21 and Heather James, *Shakespeare's Troy: Drama, Politics, and the Translation of Empire* (Cambridge: Cambridge University Press, 1997).

16 The scripting of Marcus' entry '*aloft*' in 1.1 is printed in the Folio edition of the play; and his occupation of the same space, overlooking the stage, in 5.3 is confirmed by lines 129–33. (Jonathan Bate considers the changes to stage directions made in the Folio text as likely to have playhouse authority (Introduction, 115).)

17 See further Michael Neill, *Issues of Death: Mortality and Identity in English Renaissance Tragedy* (Oxford: Clarendon Press, 1997), esp. ch. 8.

3 *Romeo and Juliet*

1 Sasha Roberts, 'Reading Shakespeare's Tragedies of Love: *Romeo and Juliet*, *Othello*, and *Antony and Cleopatra* in Early Modern England', in *A Companion to Shakespeare's Works: Vol 1 The Tragedies*, eds. Richard Dutton and Jean E. Howard (Oxford: Blackwell, 2003), 108–33.

2 Brian Gibbons, editor of the Arden edition (London and New York: Methuen, 1980), notes that the emphasis on Fortune in Shakespeare's source, Arthur Brooke's *Romeus and Juliet*, is one of Brooke's additions to his source, Boiastuau's French translation of a story by Bandello, an emphasis influenced by Chaucer's *Troilus and Criseyde* (Introduction, 36).

3 Only the first Quarto, a generally unreliable text, has 'defy'. Later Quartos and the Folio have 'deny'. Brian Gibbons, choosing the first reading, compares it with Hamlet's 'We defy augury' (5.2.215).

4 *Issues of Death*, 308–10. Neill visualises a property tomb, but the question of how the tomb is staged is problematic. The last moments of the play set the whole scene inside the tomb, at which point the audience probably sees the whole stage as the interior of the tomb and the tiring-house wall as its interior wall; but just before this point characters are evidently standing outside the tomb, looking at it, as when Paris strews flowers on Juliet's tomb or Romeo opens it (5.3). Since there is no scenic break between Romeo's opening the tomb and his entering it, it would seem that the audience's imagination has to do most of the work, since putting a property tomb on stage would create problems for the staging of the rest of the scene inside it. See also Alan Dessen, *Recovering Shakespeare's Theatrical Vocabulary* (Cambridge: Cambridge University Press, 1995), ch. 9.

4 *Julius Caesar*

1 Platter's remarks have been translated in full in Ernest Schanzer, 'Thomas Platter's Observations on the Elizabethan Stage', *Notes and Queries* 201 (1956), 465–7. Detailed arguments for the timing of the play's first performance are given in Steve Sohmer, *Shakespeare's Mystery Play: The Opening of the Globe Theatre 1599* (Manchester: Manchester University Press, 1999).

2 David Daniell, ed., *Julius Caesar* (Walton-on-Thames: Nelson, 1998), Introduction, 34–8.

3 Daniell, Introduction, 2.

4 Cynthia Marshall, 'Shakespeare, Crossing the Rubicon', *Shakespeare Survey 53* (2000), 73; John Roe, '"Character" in Plutarch and Shakespeare: Brutus, Julius Caesar, and Mark Antony', in *Shakespeare and the Classics*, eds. Charles Martindale and A. B. Taylor (Cambridge: Cambridge University Press, 2004), 173.

5 North's Plutarch is quoted from the Appendix to the Arden edition, 332.

6 'The Life of Caius Martius Coriolanus', reprinted in Appendix to *Coriolanus*, ed. Philip Brockbank (London: Methuen, 1976), 314.

7 Plutarch's account of this incident is printed on pp. 337–8 of the Appendix.

8 Coppélia Kahn, *Roman Shakespeare: Warriors, Wounds, and Women* (London: Routledge, 1997), 101.

9 Susannah Clapp in *The Observer*, Sunday 24 April 2005.

5 *Hamlet*

1 For Nashe's reference to Hamlet in 1589, see p. 9 above. Thomas Kyd, who wrote *The Spanish Tragedy*, which will figure importantly in this chapter, has been suggested as the likely author of the *Ur-Hamlet*.

2 Folio-only passages are printed in Appendix 1 of Ann Thompson and Neil Taylor's Arden edition (London: Thomson Learning, 2006). Though Q2 has nothing corresponding to this passage, there is a parallel passage on the 'humour of the children' in Q1. Roslyn Knutson summarises arguments about the dating of these observations, taking the view that the Q1 passage refers to the activities of the newly reopened children's companies in 1599–1600 and was cut from Q2, while the F passage alludes to the Blackfriars Children at a later date, perhaps 1606–8 ('Falconer to the Little Eyases', *Shakespeare Quarterly* 46 (1995), 1–31).

3 Quite how far his 'inky cloak' sets him apart is made clear by Roland Frye. Hamlet's costume is not just a black suit, but a full-length hooded garment covering the whole body. By superimposing a figure in such a costume on a picture of a courtly wedding, Frye shows how strikingly anomalous such dress renders its wearer (*The Renaissance Hamlet: Issues and Responses in 1600* (Princeton: Princeton University Press, 1984), 101).

4 Thomson and Taylor print the lines as verse, but some editors print these first few lines as prose.

5 Frye notes the clarity of church law and practice on this point. In his view the play offers no justification for Ophelia's 'maimed rites' (*Renaissance Hamlet*, 150).

6 Titus briefly asks the clown to be his messenger and Juliet converses with her nurse, but there is no earlier scene that scripts such extended and serious interaction between a tragic hero and a clown.

7 The Coventry cycle, which Shakespeare could have seen as a boy, living in Stratford, was last performed in 1579.

8 Kenneth Rothwell discusses the techniques that create this quality in the film in 'Classic Film Versions of Shakespeare's Tragedies: A Mirror for the Times', in *A Companion to Shakespeare's Works*, vol 1, *The Tragedies*, 245–6.

9 Weimann first set out his pioneering analysis of the spatial dynamics of the late medieval and early modern stage in *Shakespeare and the Popular Tradition in the Theater: Studies in the Social Dimension of Dramatic Form and Function* (Baltimore: John Hopkins University Press, 1978), and he has continued to refine it in later works. See especially *Author's Pen and Actor's Voice: Playing and Writing in Shakespeare's Theatre* (Cambridge: Cambridge University Press, 2000).

10 The history of her long representation as an aestheticised object in painting and popular culture, discussed by Elaine Showalter ('Representing Ophelia: Women, Madness, and the Responsibilities of Feminist Criticism', in *Shakespeare and the Question of Theory*, ed. Patricia Parker and Geoffrey Hartman (New York: Methuen, 1985), 77–94), is a process that surely begins with the mode of her representation within the play itself.

11 See Harold Jenkins' note to this passage in his edition for the Arden 2 series (London and New York: Methuen, 1982); and cf. Lancelot Andrewes preaching on the same theme, cited in Frye, *Renaisssance Hamlet*, 255.

12 See Robert Hapgood's note on this passage in his edition of the play for the Shakespeare in Production series (Cambridge: Cambridge University Press, 1999), 268.

6 *Othello*

1 The play is usually dated 1603–4, but Ernst Honigmann, the most recent Arden editor, dates it to 1601–2, linking it to the Moorish embassy living in London in 1600. See his *Othello* (Walton-on-Thames: Nelson, 1997), Appendix 1.

2 J. Leeds Barroll, *Politics, Plague, and Shakespeare's Theater* (Ithaca and London: Cornell University Press, 1991), 47. We do not know which plays were performed over that first Christmas; references to plays of Shakespeare's performed at court do not begin until almost two years after James' accession (Barroll, *Politics*, 119).

3 Joseph Knight and Robert Smallwood, writing respectively in 1875 and 1990, quoted in *Shakespeare in the Theatre: An Anthology of Criticism*, ed. Stanley Wells (Oxford: Oxford University Press, 2000), 113, 311.

4 Barbara Hodgdon makes this point in 'Race-ing *Othello*, Re-engendering White-out', in *Shakespeare, the Movie II: Popularising the Plays on Film, TV, and Video*, ed.

Lynda E. Boose and Richard Burt (London: Routledge, 2003), 34. Nunn's Stratford production was also filmed.

5 The quotation is from Quintilian's *Institutio Oratoria*. The Loeb translation of the fuller version of the sentence to which Rymer alludes runs as follows: 'For to embark on such tragic methods in trivial cases would be like putting the mask and buskins of Hercules on a small child' (*The Institutio Oratoria of Quintilian*, with trans. by H. E. Butler (Cambridge, Mass. and London: Heinemann, Harvard University Press, 1920–2).

6 Honigmann, Appendix 3, 378.

7 Honigmann gives a brief account of the critical history of 'double time', Introduction 68–72.

8 See further Lynda E. Boose, 'Othello's Handkerchief: "The Recognizance and Pledge of Love"', *ELR* 5 (1975), 360–74.

9 Thomas Rymer, *A Short View of Tragedy*, in *The Critical Works of Thomas Rymer*, ed. Curt A. Zimansky (New Haven: Yale University Press, 1956), 160.

10 Coleridge's famous phrase, 'the motive-hunting of motiveless malignity', occurs in a note he made in his copy of Shakespeare. Cinthio writes that '[i]t appeared marvellous to everybody that such malignity could have been discovered in a human heart' (Honigmann, ed., Appendix 3, 386).

11 Honigmann glosses these lines to mean that Emilia is nothing to Iago but someone to please his whims. It is equally possible, in my view, that the lines mean that her only intention is to please his whims. Either way, the motivation is not substantiated elsewhere in the play.

12 Alan Sinfield focuses on Desdemona to discuss the tension between coherent characterisation and the needs of the play scene by scene (*Faultlines: Cultural Materialism and the Politics of Dissident Reading* (Oxford: Clarendon Press, 1992), ch. 3).

13 The well-known phrase is Wilson Knight's, the title of chapter 5 of *The Wheel of Fire*, 4th edn (London: Methuen, 1960).

14 T. S. Eliot, '"Rhetoric" and Poetic Drama', in *Selected Essays*, 3rd edn (London: Faber and Faber, 1951), p. 39.

7 Timon of Athens

1 John Jowett discusses the collaboration very fully in the introduction to his edition of the play (Oxford: Oxford University Press, 2004), and I follow his attribution of different sections of the play throughout. See also Vickers, *Shakespeare, Co-Author*, ch. 4 and R. V. Holdsworth, 'Middleton and Shakespeare', unpublished PhD Dissertation (University of Manchester, 1982).

2 Partly because the traditional act and scene divisions added by early editors are so inappropriate in this case, and partly because H. J. Oliver's Arden edition (London: Methuen, 1976) predates so much important scholarship, I here quote from Jowett's Oxford edition of the play, which is divided into scenes only.

3 Lack of evidence cannot be used, however, as some scholars use it, to deduce that the play was not performed in Shakespeare's lifetime. Some suggestions of indirect evidence for performance are made by A. D. Nuttall (*Timon of Athens* (Hemel Hempstead: Harvester Wheatsheaf, 1989), xv) and M. C. Bradbrook (*Shakespeare the Craftsman* (Cambridge: Cambridge University Press, 1969), 165).

4 For fuller discussion of sources see Jowett, Introduction, 16–18 and for the sources themselves see *Narrative and Dramatic Sources of Shakespeare*, ed. Geoffrey Bullough, 8 vols. (New York: Columbia University Press, 1957–75), vol. 6.

5 It is probably a mistake to set too much store by early modern titles, however. The very fact that titles vary between different printed editions of the same play suggests that they functioned in a rather broad, allusive way rather than with strongly nuanced significance.

6 The phrase is the Poet's own, used in a speech that is notable for its tendency to stand outside character to comment on those who follow Timon, including the Poet himself. A Mercer is also scripted to enter, perhaps erroneously. See further Jowett's note to the opening stage direction for scene 1.

7 See Rolf Soellner, *Timon of Athens: Shakespeare's Pessimistic Tragedy* (Columbus: Ohio State University Press, 1979), 145.

8 See e.g. Bradbrook, *Shakespeare the Craftsman*, 145.

9 See Bradbrook, *Shakespeare the Craftsman*, 154–64 and Nuttall, *Timon*, 106.

10 The presence of the spade may be inferred from Apemantus' question later in the same scene: 'Why this spade?' (206). Jowett suggests that the image also recalls the gravediggers in *Hamlet* (Introduction, 66).

11 Bradbrook notes the parallels with Hospitality and Despair (*Shakespeare the Craftsman* 147, 161).

12 John W. Draper, 'The Theme of "Timon of Athens"', *Modern Language Review* 29 (1934), 21–2.

13 *Everyman*, in *Medieval Drama*, ed. Greg Walker (Oxford: Blackwell, 2000), line 396; *All For Money*, in the *Chadwyck-Healy Database of English Drama*, http://lion.chadwyck.co.uk.

14 As G. R. Hibbard points out in his introduction to the Penguin edition of the play (Harmondsworth: Penguin, 1970, 36), Marx quotes these lines in *Das Kapital* in explaining the consequences of substituting cash relationships for other kinds of human relationships.

15 Quoted in Nuttall, *Timon*, xvi–xvii.

16 Bradbrook offers this explication of Apemantus' name (*Shakespeare the Craftsman*, 157).

17 See further William Empson, *The Structure of Complex Words* (London: Chatto and Windus, 1952), ch. 7.

18 For fuller discussion of gender issues raised by the play see Coppélia Kahn, '"Magic of Bounty": Timon of Athens, Jacobean Patronage, and Maternal Power', *Shakespeare Quarterly* 38 (1987), 34–57.

19 Weimann, *Author's Pen and Actor's Voice*, 211.

20 Rhyming couplets often signal the end of a scene in Shakespeare, but one of the marks of collaboration in this play is the higher presence of rhyme.

21 This line suggests that the dishes contain stones as well as water. See Jowett's note to 11.84.

22 See further Janette Dillon, *Shakespeare and the Solitary Man* (London and Basingstoke: Macmillan, 1981) and 'Tiring House Wall Scenes at the Globe: A Change in Style and Emphasis', *Theatre Notebook* 53 (1999), 163–73.

23 Usury, the practice of extending credit at interest, was outlawed until 1571 in England, and is also closely examined through the figure of Shylock in *The Merchant of Venice*. While it remained technically illegal under the 1571 Act, the effect of the Act in practice was to establish a maximum rate of 10 per cent.

24 Jowett discusses the superfluity and conflation of epitaphs in his note to these lines.

25 As Jowett points out, this is partly a matter of authorial division, since Middleton writes most of the episodes involving the Steward. In his view, the play figures an internal dialogue between Middleton, who 'accepts the residual possibility of real friendship at the point where money no longer matters', and Shakespeare, for whom 'misanthropy makes no exceptions' ('Middleton and Debt in *Timon of Athens*', in *Money and the Age of Shakespeare*, ed. Linda Woodbridge (New York and Basingstoke: Palgrave Macmillan, 2003), 230).

8 *King Lear*

1 I quote throughout from the Quarto text as printed in René Weis' parallel-text edition (London and New York: Longman, 1993), noting important deviations between the Quarto and Folio as appropriate. R. A. Foakes' Arden edition ((Walton-on-Thames: Nelson, 1997) prints a conflated text, but clearly distinguishes lines printed in only one or other of the Quarto or Folio.

2 For fuller discussion of the status and dating of the texts see Weis' Introduction and cf. Foakes' Introduction, 110–48.

3 Some aspects of these parallels, of course, could be construed as flattering rather than offensive to James. Foakes quotes a passage from James' *Basilikon Doron*, first published in Edinburgh in 1599 and reissued in London in 1603, the year of James' accession to the English throne, in which James advises his son, 'in case it please God to provide you to all these three kingdoms', not to divide them, but to leave all three to his eldest son in order to avoid leaving 'the seed of division and discord among your posterity' (Introduction, 15). (The three kingdoms implied are England, Scotland and Wales.)

4 Charles Howard McIlwain, *The Political Works of James I: Reprinted from the Edition of 1616* (1918; rpt. New York: Russell and Russell, 1965), 272.

5 See Marie Axton, *The Queen's Two Bodies: Drama and the Elizabethan Succession* (London: Royal Historical Society, 1977), 139.

6 In the Folio text it is the Fool who speaks the answer to Lear's question: 'Lear's shadow'.

7 These lines are absent from the Folio text.

8 Edward Bond, *Lear* (London: Eyre Methuen, 1972), vii. The mock-trial of Lear's daughters (3.6.32–52) is absent from the Folio text.

9 The whole scene containing the line '[D]og-hearted daughters' (4.3) is absent from the Folio text.

10 Anthony Dawson develops this point in 'Cross-Cultural Interpretation: Reading Kurosawa Reading Shakespeare', in *A Concise Companion to Shakespeare on Screen*, ed. Diana E. Henderson (Oxford: Blackwell, 2006), 161.

11 The word 'heath', familiar as the designation of the location in so many editions of the play, is not Shakespeare's, but belongs to an editorial tradition stemming from Nicholas Rowe's edition of 1709.

12 Edmund Kean restored the tragic ending in 1823, but it was William Charles Macready who restored most of Shakespeare's text in 1838.

13 The speech in which Edgar recounts the meeting between Kent and Gloucester is present only in the Quarto.

14 These lines are spoken by Edgar in the Folio text.

9 *Macbeth*

1 The full entry on *Macbeth* is given in Kenneth Muir's Introduction to the Arden edition (9th edn (London: Methuen, 1962)), xiv–xv. Some critics have doubted the authenticity of Forman's *Book*; see further John Wilders, ed., *Macbeth*, Plays in Production (Cambridge: Cambridge University Press, 2004), 2, n.1

2 Muir discusses this context more fully in his Introduction, xvi–xix, quoting Hotson's account of Shakespeare's personal acquaintance with some of the Gunpowder Plot conspirators. 'Equivocation', as practised by those on trial, was an ambiguous form of words seeking to avoid stating the truth while technically not lying. The term was in use before 1606, as Hamlet's response to the gravedigger's quibbling precision shows (*Hamlet* 5.1.133–4).

3 Muir, Introduction, lx.

4 Muir, Appendix A, 178.

5 Muir, Appendix A, 179.

6 Wilders, ed., *Macbeth*, 115.

7 Quoted by Muir, Introduction, lxviii.

8 The strong traces of Seneca in *Macbeth* have often been noted. See eg Robert S. Miola, *Shakespeare and Classical Tragedy: The Influence of Seneca* (Oxford: Clarendon Press, 1992), ch. 3 and Yves Peyré, '"Confusion now hath made his masterpiece": Senecan resonances in *Macbeth*', in *Shakespeare and the Classics*, eds. Martindale and Taylor, 141–55.

9 Simon Williams, 'The Tragic Actor', in *The Cambridge Companion to Shakespeare on Stage*, eds. Stanley Wells and Sarah Stanton (Cambridge: Cambridge University Press: 2002), 123.

10 Wilders notes that it was omitted by Kemble, Macready, Charles Kean, Irving and Forbes-Robertson (*Macbeth*, 178). Davenant includes the discussion of Macduff's flight and the Messenger, but excludes both Lady Macduff's son and the arrival of the murderers.

11 An anonymous Lord informs Lenox of the reason for Macduff's departure at 3.6.29–37. Both spectators and readers sometimes miss this point, however. In Holinshed Macduff leaves Scotland after the murder of his family in order to seek revenge.

12 Emrys Jones has argued further that the emotion released by the slaughter of Macduff's children is important in opening the way to tragic sympathy for Macbeth himself in the final act of the play (*Scenic Form*, 221).

13 The Quarto text of *King Lear* is over 3000 lines long. Others, however, such as *The Tempest* and *A Midsummer Night's Dream*, are barely longer than *Macbeth*.

14 See Neill, *Issues of Death*, 205.

10 *Antony and Cleopatra*

1 Joan Rees, 'An Elizabethan Eyewitness of *Antony and Cleopatra*', *Shakespeare Survey* 6 (1953), 91.

2 See further Alvin Kernan, *Shakespeare the King's Playwright: Theater in the Stuart Court* (New Haven: Yale University Press, 1995), 121–7 and Heather James, *Shakespeare's Troy: Drama, Politics, and the Translation of Empire* (Cambridge: Cambridge University Press, 1997), 147.

3 The terminology of acts is purely one of convenience for reference to Wilders' edition. The Folio, which is the only extant text, has no act division and does not even number scenes. Emrys Jones makes a strong case for the play as dividing naturally into two parts, with the break in the middle of what modern editions call Act 3 (*Scenic Form*, 225–30).

4 *Plutarch's Lives of Coriolanus, Caesar, Brutus, and Antonius in North's Translation*, ed. R. H. Carr (Oxford: Clarendon Press, 1906), 164.

5 *Plutarch's Lives*, 186.

6 Janet Adelman has argued very persuasively for the play as answering the bitterness of *Timon* with a positive vision of male bounty that 'reaches toward a new kind of masculinity' by incorporating the female (*Suffocating Mothers: Fantasies of Maternal Origin in Shakespeare's Plays, Hamlet to the Tempest* (New York and London: Routledge, 1992), 190).

7 This pervasive theatricality may also have a topical dimension. As Heather James puts it: 'In *Antony and Clepatra*, Shakespeare's theater is engrossed by the notion of playing to a court that is itself increasingly mimicking the theater, in masques or in the sometimes farcical scenes performed in court' (*Shakespeare's Troy*, 148).

11 *Coriolanus*

1 Cecil is quoted in Lee Bliss's edition of the play (Cambridge: Cambridge University Press, 2000), Introduction, 32.
2 The Folio, containing the only extant early text, is generally thought, partly on the evidence of the stage directions, to be close to Shakespeare's 'foul papers' (his uncorrected working manuscript). Stage directions in printed texts are not necessarily authorial; they may reflect playhouse input.
3 More precisely, Shakespeare conflates several riots against usury and food shortages in Plutarch into one here.
4 See further Annabel Patterson, *Shakespeare and the Popular Voice* (Oxford: Basil Blackwell, 1989), 136–9.
5 Shakespeare Birthplace Trust Records Office, Misc. Doc. I, 106. See also S. Schoenbaum, *William Shakespeare: A Compact Documentary Life* (Oxford: Oxford University Press, 1977), 236–7.
6 *Brecht on Theatre*, ed. and trans. John Willett, 2nd edn (London: Methuen, 1974), 257. See also Margot Heinemann, 'How Brecht Read Shakespeare', in *Political Shakespeare: New Essays in Cultural Materialism*, eds. Jonathan Dollimore and Alan Sinfield (Manchester: Manchester University Press, 1985), 202–30.
7 Shakespeare's Martius enters the gates of Corioles alone, but Plutarch's enters 'with very few men to help him' (Plutarch is quoted from the Appendix to Brockbank's Arden edition, 322.)
8 Philip Brockbank assigns this line to 'All', but it is assigned to Martius in the Folio.
9 Brockbank, Introduction, 80.
10 Laurence Kitchin, quoted in Wells, *Shakespeare in the Theatre*, 265.
11 Adelman, *Suffocating Mothers*; Stanley Cavell, *Disowning Knowledge in Seven Plays of Shakespeare*, 2nd edn (Cambridge: Cambridge University Press, 2003); Kahn, *Roman Shakespeare*.
12 Cavell, *Disowning Knowledge*, 145.
13 Adelman, *Suffocating Mothers*, 148.
14 *Coriolanus*, unlike the tragedies so far discussed, may have been written in acts, and as such may have been the first of Shakespeare's tragedies specifically intended for the indoor Blackfriars Theatre, where act divisions were necessary to allow time for trimming the candles. This suggestion is made by Lee Bliss in her introduction (p. 4). On act division generally, see ch. 2, n. 2 above.
15 Brockbank, Appendix, 343.
16 Brockbank, Appendix, 314.

Index